ARCHITECTURAL SCALE

ARCHITECTURAL SCALE

Heath Licklider

GEORGE BRAZILLER

NEW YORK

CONTENTS

Scale

After you have spent long hours at the drawing board imagining and describing a building there is nothing so exciting as to see it under construction. In sunlight, the qualities that you have planned come to life with a drama that is always surprising; and as you walk around and within the structure, a thousand lines, planes, and masses for the first time subtly shift or wheel in grand formation. A manufacturer may derive as much satisfaction when he sees his products begin to roll off the assembly line. A dramatist probably experiences a similar enjoyment when his characters and situations come to life on the stage. But the special pleasure of reshaping a portion of the world stage is reserved for the architect. His designs take their place with the other realities of the environment – with older buildings, masses of trees, city streets and ploughed fields – as the background of life as it is lived.

Following a building from the paper design, through the organized chaos of construction to its completion, is as instructive as it is exciting. It is the designer's only reliable way of checking the accuracy of his anticipations, and it is the final test of the design that he imagined. The wall that he imagined as heartily rough, may appear rough with a knuckle-scraping hostility in the executed building. The railing that was to be silky smooth to the touch may turn out to have the greased feel of a fireman's pole. Colours that were seductively combined in sample chips may have an entirely different impact in the large; and shapes that were handsome in the flat may lose, rather than gain, by realization in the round. But size and relationships of size are the qualities that are most apt to be distorted in the process of blowing up a design from a sketch to an executed building.

In my own modest designs, for example, there is a small but consistent error in the anticipation of spaces and sizes. When I visit the completed building I am surprised – and often delighted

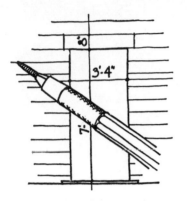

Sizes that I accurately
represented in my drawings

that were accurately
constructed

as I imagined them

as they appeared

– to discover that corridors, that I had thought too narrow, are sufficiently roomy, and that walls, that I had feared would be cluttered with fussy details, are bold and big enough to take the treatment. What is involved here is usually called scale. It embraces a complex of factors. There are the actual sizes that I accurately represented in my drawings and were accurately constructed – so many feet high and so many feet long. There are the apparent sizes, as I imagined them and as they appeared when the building was constructed. And there are relationships between sizes: between apparent sizes and actual sizes, and between sizes as imagined and sizes as they are actually seen. I suppose the unexpected roominess and extra size in my work is an expression of a tendency akin to mild claustrophobia – fear of closed places. And where an error of this kind is allowed to creep into a design, a small part of the building becomes accidental, rather than planned.

The chances of such an error, and of other mistakes in anticipating sizes, are greatly increased by the rapidly changing unfamiliar vocabulary of our architecture. When an architectural style is well established, or slowly evolving, living among its buildings provides a natural school for the designer. Surrounded by an architectural vocabulary, he easily acquires the ability to anticipate its often-seen effects. But the buildings of Modern Architecture that might provide such an education are few and scattered. We are without a sure familiar vocabulary at just the time when the dimensions of construction have acquired a magnitude never demanded before; and it is obvious that the larger the project is the easier it is to fall into errors of size and relationship of size.

The schools of architecture may be expected to find new means to counteract these circumstances. But academic study has its own hazards. The careful checking of imagined sizes against real ones is easily neglected while students are learning rapidly through the study of projects that will never be built. Basic mistakes in anticipation and imagination may become ingrained during the experience of dozens of paper projects. And they may even train the mind to the habit of overlooking the difference between paper effects and real ones. As a rule, when an architectural student's teacher first peers over his shoulder and says that his design is 'out of scale', it is the beginning of a long series of exasperating experiences. With a little study a student becomes increasingly aware of sizes and relationships of size and increasingly perplexed by their maladjustment in his own designs. But he is not likely to receive an explanation of scale that will enable him to cope easily with his mistakes. Indeed, the student whose teacher draws his attention to scale problems is one of the fortunate ones. In the present state of architectural education his critic may have responded to the obscurities of scale by retreating from the subject altogether. One reason for this is almost farcical. 'Scale' stands for a series of recurring problems of size which have extremely varied origins in design. To attempt a single explanation is self-defeating. For all practical purposes the unqualified word is useful only

9

as a vague generic term; and unless this is understood, discussions of scale become entangled in the futile task of seeking a single explanation for what are, in fact, very diverse phenomena.

Yet of all the aspects of visual design that have been singled out for special attention, scale has been given a remarkably consistent billing near the top. Alberti's great treatise of 1485 requires that 'in number size and situation the parts of a design answer each other, be matched, balanced and set out with the greatest care.'[1] The grand masters of the Ecole des Beaux Arts have grappled with its problems with varying degrees of success; and André Lurçat – the latest of them, if he cares for the title – is most illuminating on the subject.[2] Even in the clean sweep of the Bauhaus period, which favoured a 'science of vision' that was to be, Walter Gropius was able to write that 'if design is to be a specific language of communication for the expression of subconscious ideas, then it must have its own elementary codes of scale, form, and colour':[3] thus giving scale a place in a basic triumvirate of visual design. That it is not generally well understood, and a student should commonly receive little help with it, is largely owing to the failure to develop cumulative or comprehensive theories of design in architecture. And this shortcoming, let me hasten to add, has advantages as well as disadvantages.

Picasso 1937

or Titian 1537

[1] Leone Battista Alberti, *Architectura, Joseph James Leoni Translation* (1726), Joseph Rykwert, editor, London, 1955, Book 14, Chap. VIII, p. 202.
[2] André Lurcat, *Formes Compositions et Lois d'Harmonie*, Paris, 1955, Vol. 4.
[3] Walter Gropius, 'Design Topics', *Magazine of Art*, Dec. 1947.

A building by Vanbrugh . . .

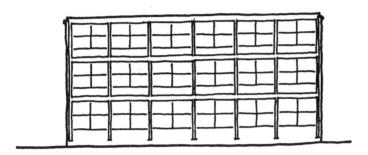

to one by Mies

There is no progress in art, of course. You may prefer a painting by Picasso 1937 to one by Titian 1537 or a building by Vanbrugh to one by Mies; but there is no reason to suppose that one or the other will be a better work of art because of its date. The same observation may be made of theories of art insofar as they apply to the creation of works of art. This was best illustrated, I think, by Sir Donald Francis Tovey who compared theories of art – music in this case – to the strings upon which the crystals of rock candy are formed.[4] When the crystals have formed from the sugar water, the string is no longer of any importance; and when a building is completed, the theories that helped the architect

[4] Donald Francis Tovey, *A Musician Talks, Vol.* 1, *The Integrity of Music,* London, 1941, p. 84.

11

while designing it are no longer valuable. The crystalline structure of the rock candy, in the one instance, and the inherent arrangement of the building, in the other, constitute the most valid 'theory' of the design – the description that best explains what it is.

What has been written and explained about scale is still, to a great extent, entwined with the superfluous strands of obsolete theories. Any investigation of the subject must encounter a very strange bag of tricks indeed: whirling squares and pentagrams, harmonic ratios, column-drum modules, an army of little men stretching themselves uncomfortably within circles, and that durable pair, beauty and unity. It is not surprising that a busy architect may fail to see the relevance of all of this to his work as it is actually conducted, and we can sympathize with him when he rejects the whole debris. But theory has another, more hopeful, side. This is the construction of an understanding of the facts and circumstances relevant to designing in general. Unlike art, and theories of creation, this kind of an understanding can progress from the narrow grasp of a few factors – which leaves most of the field unintelligible – through broader and broader understanding, to a wide comprehension that brings the major factors into a single coherence. The progress that is achieved in this way is the expansion of the field of comprehensive understanding from which the architect is free to shape as he pleases all, or any part, to the service of his designs.

The history of architectural scale, as a subject to be explored, is almost a textbook illustration of the great difficulty of building up a cumulative understanding when, at every analysis, it is hitched to the shooting star of a living work of art. Baby has not only been thrown out with the bath water, he has been sent down the drain with every change of creative climate. Cumulative gains in the understanding of scale have also tended to be limited by its 'newness' as a field of study. In this respect, the study of scale has something in common with modern psychology. People have always had their psychologies, needless to say; and I would guess that there are few important facts about the workings of the human mind that are not described or implied in the Book of Proverbs. Yet modern psychology can be said to originate with Sigmund Freud, for he made it possible to study the personality as it is formed, free from preconceptions as to what it ought to be, or how it ought to function. Architectural scale has also always existed; and there are few problems of scale that have not been superbly solved in the monuments of the past by architects who were primarily interested in symbolism, in proportional systems, in utility, or in absolute standards of beauty. But the study of architectural scale has been consciously undertaken only recently, stimulated by a growing awareness of the dependence of man's experiences upon his own aptitudes and limitations. Scale treatment probably originates in attempts to attain practical and occult objectives that now seem almost extra-architectural. The possibility of studying scale for the qualities that it can directly contribute to designing, has had to wait upon the rise of a keen curiosity about the subjective aspects of visual experience. Even now, the subject is so far from a synthesis of the valuable insights that have been gained that it encompasses at least three somewhat contradictory points of view toward size and relationships of size. These may be called the physical, proportional, and human conceptions of scale. Of the three, human scale fully allows for the subjective experiencing of architecture. And it is human scale that appears to offer, for the first time, a realistic basis for the consolidation of what we know, and the beginning of a cumulatively built-up analysis of scale.

If the study of scale is to be useful, it obviously must be compatible with the architect's approach to his creative work. But the thoughtful architect is increasingly impressed with the example of the natural sciences, and he increasingly demands that analyses of architectural problems be not only useful but also reasonably comprehensive of application. We may assume that he requires a description of scale that will be applicable to the buildings of the past as well as to those of the present – although it need not resurrect the preconceptions of past architects – that it should be compatible with what is known about related areas of study – aesthetics and psychology in particular – and that it should remain useful throughout the flurried changes of the creative climate.

The first step, and my primary purpose, is to place in the hands of architectural students a description of scale that will help them to discover the complex relationship between the lines that they draw on paper, the same divisions as they stand full-size upon the site, and the experience that they may afford an observer. That the job needs to be done, is illustrated by the number of buildings that entirely lack the visual interest that is generated by a careful adjustment of relationships of size. The urgency of the need is evinced by our inadequacy in the face of the mounting problems of scale provoked by traffic engineering, urban concentration, and the sprawl of our residential suburbs. The problems of design will remain. They can only be worked out in designing. But they may be faced with greater discernment, and more easily solved, when we know what they are likely to be and what is likely to control them in designing. We shall begin by examining separately physical, proportional, and human scale – with an eye to what is of special value in each approach – and we shall develop the conception of human scale further, as the proper basis for an understanding of architectural scale in our time.

Physical Scale

A recurring conviction that the practical arrangement of a building is the proper basis for its visual scale does not require high-flown theoretical premises. It is confirmed whenever a designer realistically attempts to control the exact way that a building is put together. Probably no one has ever constructed a building, or made working drawings for one, who has not at some point in the work been annoyed by the awkward way that some of the materials fit into their positions in section and plan. The sheer variety of the units that must be fitted together is staggering. It includes the working structure, from the largest girders and columns to the smallest bolts or nails; the enclosing shell, from bricks to window and door assemblies; and the visceral entanglements of pipes, wiring, and ducts. Each part has a size determined more or less by convenience in erection, by its function, by the manufacturing process, or by the nature of the material that it is made from. And for each building a full set of dimensions must be found, by trial and error or from past experience, which is everywhere suited to the sizes of the parts from which it is constructed.

The reasons for the size of a building unit are seldom simple. A brick is dimensioned so that it can be grasped and lifted by the mason in one hand; but its length and height also represent a compromise between the size large enough to be firm and rapidly laid up, and one small enough to prevent excessive warping in firing and cracking in handling. The final adjustment in size was made recently (in the U.S.) to fit the brick into a four inch modular grid. Ease of erection influences the design of many industrially produced wall panels, which are made sufficiently small and light to be easily handled by two men. But it is also important that the panels be large enough to minimize the problems of jointing. The catalogue of steel shapes that are available for building includes the I-sections, channels, and angles, that are among the most

15

efficient structural sections; but these are also the shapes that can be manufactured in a rolling mill. To explain adequately even the simplest of the materials and parts that make up a building, requires a short history of its origins, it uses, and its process of manufacture. And in many instances, it also requires the explanation of a widespread customary usage that has frozen it into an arbitrary shape and size. Each material and each prefabricated part has either a fixed range of sizes, or a conventional size, or a range of sizes that will cause problems if they are surpassed. The designer is dealing not so much with feet and inches as with the predetermined or narrowly circumscribed sizes of materials and parts.

The inherent limitations that the sizes of architectural materials have always carried with them are becoming more and more precisely defined in our time. Even in the past – when building materials were almost directly exploited from nature – designs for wood never entirely escaped the dimensions of the log and wood graining, and designs for stone never entirely escaped from the dimensions of its geological formation. Nevertheless, much of the time a designer might reasonably consider that he was shaping materials with consistencies and traits rather than set dimensions.

With consistencies and traits
rather than set dimensions

The limitations now tend to be more specific, as most materials are industrially produced in quantity and manufactured in precisely shaped standard units. If a building is to be easily fabricated and if its divisions are to be built into it – rather than merely applied to it – they must accommodate the sizes and divisions of the materials from which it is constructed. Fitting them together is simplified where all of the parts are made in modular sizes; and considerable progress has been made in this direction. But even

16

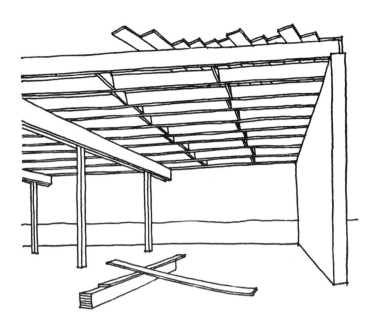

The roof sheathing may be thin and the girders designed for uniform loading

in a completely modular structure, each material and each part finds its position in the regulating grid of sizes according to the size that, for a complex of reasons, it 'wants' to assume.

A larger, more conspicuous, unit of physical measure is supplied by a building's structural system. Structural logic lays down the rules for a kind of puzzle-game. The architect is permitted the widest latitude to determine any part of the system as he sees fit. But for every choice that he makes, there is corresponding pressure to reshape the whole structure so that it may perform its tasks efficiently. In a wood building, for example, the designer may choose to create a roof with light joists closely spaced, with heavy joists spaced wide apart, or with no joists at all. And there may be excellent non-structural reasons for any of these choices. But it inevitably follows, with the first choice, that the roof sheathing may be thin and the girders designed for uniform loading throughout their length. With the second choice, it follows that the sheathing must be heavier and that the girders must be figured for the concentrated loads of the widely spaced rafters. With the

17

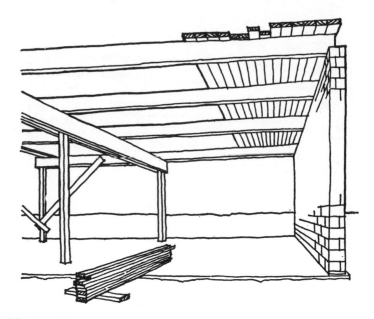

The sheathing must be heavier and the girders figured for the concentrated loads

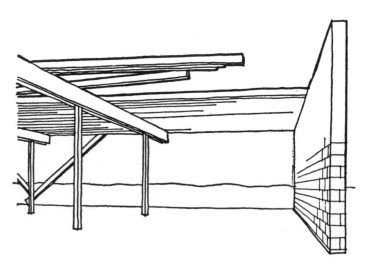

The roof sheathing must be very heavy indeed

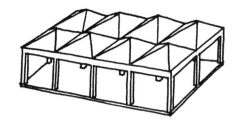

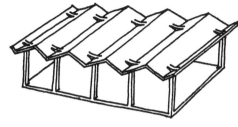

Shells, vaults or folded planes may easily provide a unit that is an eighth or a quarter of a small building

third choice, the roof sheathing must be very heavy indeed and, as in the first case, the girders will be uniformly loaded. In this fashion not only the rafters, but all of the members that are affected by the designer's choice, respond to the puzzle-like influence of structural relationships.

Throughout the working structure, this kind of interaction introduces an order of dimensions that is as remorselessly present in steel or reinforced concrete as it is in wood. Each variation in structural design has its price, either in efficiency, or in a corresponding rearrangement of all of the members affected. This discipline invariably provides the architect with a series of physical dimensions that must be fitted together with the other parts of the building. Where there is a structural skeleton of columns and beams, it supplies a large module running throughout the design. Where the structural units are shells, vaults, or folded concrete planes, they may easily provide a unit that is an eighth or a quarter of a small building. And where a single shell or vault embraces the whole building, all of its divisions will necessarily be related to the structural span. Can there be any doubt that structural behaviour and systems of construction determine orders of physical dimensions that are, as a rule, the natural bases for a building's visual scale?

19

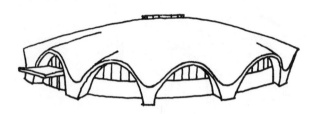

When a single shell embraces the whole building all dimensions will necessarily be related to the structural span

The discipline of planning is as exacting as that of construction. It is tangibly expressed in the walls, partitions, floor levels, and furniture arrangements of a building; and it invisibly measures and allocates the useful space. The intimate dimensions for human use, for example those of stair treads, railings, doors and furniture, form a special class. If stair risers, railings, or cabinets are too high, the occupant not only may be surprised at their appearance, but in order to use them he will be required to stretch himself uncomfortably. Thus the dimensions that people actually touch are not only seen but are also intimately felt. Where a work space is custom-fitted, as is the modern kitchen or bath room, the accommodation of people's bodies and bodily movements fills the room with dimensions that – within an inch or two – are determined by use. And combinations of these dimensions set the efficient over-all dimension for the room. The more intimately and carefully a building is designed for the activities of its occupants, the more these measurements determine its minimum dimensions. In a highly functional building, such as a school or a hospital, the snowballing effect of these functional space requirements is impressive.[5]

In the design of a classroom the space required for the student's comfort, for the teacher, for the best relationship between teacher and student, and for adequate lighting, establishes the room unit and the arrangement within it, with considerable rigour. In a hospital room, or ward, the spaces for the hygienic placement of the patients' beds, for ventilation, and for convenience in nursing, establish the room unit with little latitude for the free manipulation of its size or its shape. In either a school

---

[5] Professor Rasmussen (see n.p. 23) refers to Kaare Klint's (1918–54) studies of useful plan dimensions.

or a hospital, the efficient width of a wing of the building must be made up of useful combinations of these rooms, and of other rooms that are equally predetermined. The economical functioning of elevators, air-conditioning and plumbing, place other sets of preferred dimensions upon the plans. Out of doors, the orientation of the interiors to the sun, to the wind, and for quiet and for privacy, and the requirements for parking areas and access drives, impose further limitations upon the disposition of space. In short, the investigation that precedes the design of either a school or a hospital building may easily determine – within fairly narrow limits – all of the rough dimensions and shapes of the building. And the discipline of these dimensions, which are generated in making the space useful, can be relaxed only at an increased cost to the clients, or at the price of less efficiency in the operation of the institution. Achieving a judicious balance between this influence and others that make the building valuable is one of the architect's unique skills.

It is clear that practical designing is conducted within a framework of preordained sizes of plan arrangement, of materials, and of structural elements. Some of them are fixed absolutely, others are determined within narrow limits, and many are only loosely indicated. The architect must be impressed by the existence of this network of limitations, and he must look for their co-ordination. To build at all, a way must be found to accommodate most of them. To build well, the designer must find a way of building that synthesizes them, so that each element of the design meets several of the requirements. In a good design the structural system, for example, may not only be efficiently designed in itself, but it also may help in the division of the useful space and may be especially suited to the building material that is used.

The synthesis of physical dimensions often finds its expression in a bay unit. In a medieval hall, for instance, the synthesizing bay unit may co-ordinate a useful plan area, a handsome visual division, and a convenient structural unit for stone vaulting and large window openings. In a modern office building, the bay may be even more comprehensive. It may provide a suitable unit of steel skeleton construction and a useful area of rental space; and it may also allow the space to be divided in many ways by a modular partition system and furnish an elaborate system of lighting and air-conditioning.

In the purely practical design of buildings, the many physical divisions that are established and co-ordinated into practical syn-

The visual scale may lose much of its effect because of its synthetic relationship to the practical design

theses, provide a measure of a design that – when it is seen – is likely to be emphatic. Often the visual scale of a building will be based upon these divisions. And when it is not, it may lose much of its effect because of its synthetic relationship to the practical design. For where the practical synthesis of the design is seen and understood by a spectator, it endows the visual scale treatment with a double significance that can be acquired in no other way. The unit of size which engages the eye can also tell the spectator about the materials and method of fabrication, and even about the life that goes on within the building. Thus the clapboards of a colonial house, the lichened stones of a medieval church, and the corrugations of a cement-asbestos roof furnish the visual scale of the building with small divisions, and the same divisions help to convey the nature of the materials. The flying arcs of concrete shells and the neat sweeps of steel girders not only provide vigorous divisions for the eye, they illustrate very different principles of construction. The open cage of a loft building, the long windows spaced between stacks of a library, and the floor levels and stair towers of an office building, mark grand subdivisions of a building's shape and, at the same time, convey considerable intelligence about the human activities that are its reason for being.

Visual units of this kind are not planted on a building, but built into it. Many of them, such as the repeating shapes of the structural bays, may be found on one side of a building, may run through the interior, and may be rediscovered on the other side. Others, such as masonry units, wall panels, and paving blocks, may appear and reappear throughout a design. In each case, the fact that the visual statement seems to be a necessary part of the building, or that it occurs throughout the structure, lends it an added authority. Consequently, it is inevitable that an architect who is interested in the way that his building is put together should come to recognize the special value of these phsyical dimensions in the treatment of a building's scale. And it is not surprising that some architects have decided that they are the natural measuring system of architecture which, very directly, should be the basis for its treatment of visual scale.

This approach to architectural scale does not have a long history. As a consciously held attitude, it may have originated in the romantic conception of the art of the Middle Ages that was developed in the late nineteenth century, that descended into the arts and crafts movements, and from there – in the company of many influential notions – into modern architecture. Its most recent statement was made, with mild good sense, by Professor Rasmussen in *Experiencing Architecture*.[6] However, we may observe that whether it is recognized by the designer or not, the idea of physical scale almost inevitably accompanies a purist approach to designing; and that traces of it are found wherever suitability is a criterion of visual design – that is to say, in all but the most pastry-like buildings.

The rigorous synthesis of practical and aesthetic elements that marks the designs of Mies, or of the Smithsons, clearly makes it inevitable that scale, as well as other visual qualities, shall be very directly derived from the shapes and sizes of the practical synthesis. And when a real eloquence is achieved, as in the recent buildings of Louis Kahn, the appearance of the building is not only derived directly from the structural system and materials, but they are just as clearly designed for appearance as well as for function. Consequently, it is often very difficult to determine which is the truck and which the trailer. If these nearly perfect

---

[6] Steen Eiler Rasmussen, 'Scale and Proportion', *Experiencing Architecture*, London, 1959 (Cambridge, Mass., 1962), p. 105.

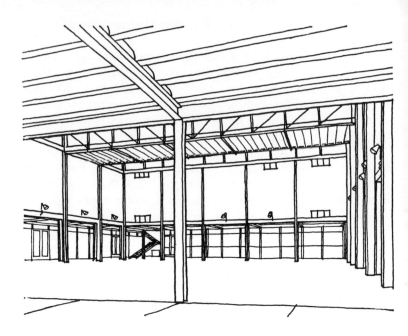

*The rigorous synthesis of practical and aesthetic elements makes it
inevitable that scale shall be very directly derived from the shapes
and sizes of the practical synthesis*

syntheses often seem to be achieved at the price of a very gen-
eralized space arrangement, which minimizes the specific requirements for human use, this is defensible and even desirable for
some programmes.

The academic purists of the beginning of the nineteenth century did not go so far; but their refinements led in a similar
direction – toward a near correspondence of the visual and practical divisions of the design. Compared to the other buildings of the
day, those of Soufflot or of Soane, tend to be stripped of superfluous ornaments. The working columns, arches, and walls, and
the block shapes derived from major plan divisions, furnish the
armature of the visual arrangement. At the other extreme, when
the Beaux Arts school was at the height of its influence, and
architects were not conspicuously aware of the close relationship
between a building's appearance and its construction, there was a
lingering respect for suitability. The main visual divisions of a
building tended to be pavilions, engaged porticos, or ornamental

bays – representing the wings, courts, and important rooms behind the façade – and those practical elements of the building
which could be used to indicate use and specific character – such
as studio windows, stable doors, or stage towers – were often
eagerly exploited in the visual design. All in all, we may safely
generalize that architects will become conscious of physical scale,
to some degree, whenever their paper designs are based upon
realities of construction and use. And in our time there are few
architects who do not appreciate the additional authority that
function lends to visual statements.

The major criticisms of physical scale should be directed toward the assumption that it is a complete and sufficient conception. For while few excellent buildings have been designed without some trace of this approach to scale, even fewer have followed
it exclusively. The reason for this lies in the important difference
between a physical order – based upon the practical dimensions
for materials, structural system, and space arrangement – and the
visual impression that it conveys. In some instances the practical
order is hidden from view, in others it is seen but conveys no
corresponding visual order, and in still other cases what is seen is
misleading.

It is often inconvenient to expose all of the materials from
which a building is constructed. In most theatres, for example, a
cocoon of lighting galleries, quiet lobbies, ventilating chambers,
and recording or broadcasting rooms, must be wrapped around
the audience, hiding the materials of the exterior walls and roof.
In a simpler design, such as a private residence, the architect may
eschew all revetments and use a single set of materials for the
exterior and for all of the rooms of the interior. But if the set of
materials is to be everywhere satisfactory, the choice of materials
will be very limited; and the designer frequently prefers to cover
one material with another that is especially chosen for wearing,
acoustical, or weathering properties. Even where a material is
exposed to view, some of the dimensions that are important to its
function may be hidden. Reinforced concrete has, in physical fact,
an intricate and elegant measure of size and stress provided by
the reinforcing bars that are everywhere adjusted and bent to
meet the stresses. If they could be seen, they would almost automatically provide the visual scale treatment with a telling ingredient. But it is the impassive concrete surface that meets the eye;
and it is the over-all thicknesses and shapes of the members that

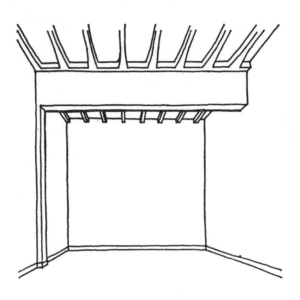

*The spectator may see a fragment of what is a complete and
balanced structural order*

carry the full burden of communication. Half of the puzzle-game
of stresses is concealed inside. To a lesser degree, the same lack of
candour exists in a simple brick wall. It is ordinarily the surface
that dominates the visual impressions. The face of the bricks is
seen and contributes a valuable unit of measure; but the thicknesses of the wall are hidden. Yet it is the thickness of the brick
and the depth of the wall, at every point, which determines the
physical value of the enclosure. It is only when the thickness is
repeatedly brought to view in wall ends, in piers, and in openings
in the wall, that this essential fact of its size is apparent to a spectator.

Obviously it is sometimes as inconvenient to expose the structural system as it is to show all of the materials. Indeed, adequate
fire and weather protection may make its concealment mandatory.
Furthermore, it should be appreciated that although a continuous
system of construction divides the whole building into regular
bays, it may be seen in a fragmentary way. What is shown on
most exteriors is an edge of the structural system. This may be
self-explanatory – as concrete columns, beams and girders often
are – or it may reveal very little of the order that is behind it. The

side view of a long-span building, for example, may convey no hint of the closely spaced columns of the end sides. Similarly, many concrete shell and folded plane bays reach the edge of the building as uncommunicative beam or slab shapes. And inside a building, unless the room divisions rigidly adhere to the structural bays, the spectator may see only a fragment of what is, in physical actuality, a complete and balanced structural order. One column and a girder that rests one end on it, while the other end plunges through a partition, contributes little either to visual order or to scale. The physical measure contributed by a structural system cannot be counted on to control automatically an observer's experience of sizes. Most of the time, it is a resource that must be deliberately and skilfully nurtured by the designer in order to yield its full value.

Much the same relationship exists between visual scale and the practical divisions of the plan. Rooms buried in the interior of a building, can contribute their order to the exterior only when they are represented by other shapes, or when they are raised above the surrounding rooms. The diminution of corridor widths, corresponding to the traffic that they carry, may show a fine logic when it is seen in plan. But to an observer walking within them, the changes of shape may appear as meaningless bulges in the

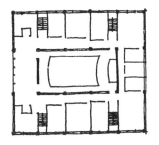

Rooms buried in the interior can contribute only when they are represented by other shapes or raised above the surrounding rooms

27

walls. Perhaps the most striking illustration of the way that the physical ordering of a plan may fail to provide a corresponding visual order is provided by a large multi-story apartment house. Each floor may be admirably laid out in compact efficient apartments of several kinds; but when these divisions are expressed on the exterior, they provide a visual disorder that in no way represents the logic of the interior arrangement.

We may observe, then, that while the physical divisions of materials, structural systems and plan arrangements may often be directly exploited in a building's scale treatment, this can be done only when physical actuality and visual impression coincide, or when the designer creates a satisfactory relationship between them. It is, after all, a little naive to suppose that when a building's physical make-up is merely shown it will be properly understood without the intervention of familiarity or of some analogy with a customary arrangement. Where programme, materials, and construction are new to the spectator, the physical actuality of the building may afford little to which the eye can attach a size. The Martian forms of the new rocket launching stations, and the Babylonian piles of the atomic plants, are mysterious shapes. The size of these new building types is only appreciated by the men who work in and around them. And, to a lesser degree, all innovations in plan arrangement or in building technology tend to create problems of scale until they have been incorporated into an architectural vocabulary that is at least somewhat familiar. We may expect that the familiarity will be provided partly by the spectator's repeatedly experiencing the design and partly by the designer's shaping it to fit the human mind and emotions. At present, there is an army of these homeless materials and structural units – incompletely assimilated into the architectural vocabulary and, as often as not, deceptive in size.

The difference between the mere existence in fact of a physical system of measure and the perception of it, does not permit the designer to leave the observer's visual impressions of size to a chance correspondence between fact and appearance. And if scale – to this extent – must be consciously studied as a visual problem, we must ask if a strict adherence to physical scale does not unnecessarily deprive the architect of opportunities to exploit impressions of size expressively. For the practical synthesis of the design not only can be effectively expressed through the visual treatment, but it can also be given its final quality of largeness or smallness. Under the circumstances, it is not surprising to find that physical scale is usually expanded to include additional conceptions of scale, which attempt to control a spectator's impressions of size through a system of proportions, or through directly designing for his visual experience. But these complications should not obscure the vital relationship between physical actuality and visual impressions that is inherent in the physical conception of scale. For if it is not always convenient or desirable to consider it a rigid requirement, there is an important reason for departing from it with caution. To say that there should be a very direct relationship between appearance and reality is, after all, to point the way to sanity.

Proportional Systems

One way that the practical arrangement of a design may be modified to make it more satisfactory to the eye is easily observed while driving through the countryside. Some barns are strictly utilitarian, with a visual order that is the by-product of an efficient way of building – practical doors for cattle, louvres for ventilation and ramps for wagon access. In other barns additional care has been taken to refine the shapes and to regularize the spacing of windows and posts; colour has been used to snap out some shapes and to suppress others; and the roof ventilators have been crowned with obelisks – of all shapes! This casual dressing up of a practical design is often successful where a building's materials, construction and plan can remain loosely synthesized. But one has only to glance at the ribbed shells of a Gothic choir and radiating chapels, or at the severities of a Mies pavilion, to know that the spare regularity of these buildings is more demanding, and that their visual refinement must be accomplished through a system of shapes that is fittingly exact. For buildings with a tight and regular physical order it is natural for the designer to seek a matching order of divisions and relationships for the eye; and one way to do this is through a visual proportional system.

The close connection between the practical order of a building and its visual design should not lead us to suppose that proportional systems have usually originated in the refinement of utilitarian designs. The functional requirements of most of the great monuments of the architectural past have not been pressing; and the architect has considered them much less important than the expression of intangible ideas and emotions. What he has considered important to express in them is often very difficult for us to appreciate. Buildings have been laid out to conform to magical formulae, or to represent astrological patterns, in the expectation that the resulting shapes would help to control natural and supernatural forces. Buildings have been designed so that the whole scheme, or large parts of it, is symbolic of the ideas valued by the culture. At the same time, architects have sought to make their designs expressive – to enable the spectator to recognize emotions in the shapes and in their relationships to each other.

Reviewing the past it is often difficult, or impossible, to discover what part of a building's appearance the architect intended to be seen, what part was the by-product of long forgotten occult arrangements, or what part derived from a happy facility for combining these intentions. In the temples and tombs of ancient Egypt, for example, most of what we see appears to have been designed for non-visual reasons. These people buried some of their most delightful painted rooms under the sand, and placed some of their handsomest bas-reliefs on walls that were hardly illuminated. In the finest Japanese architecture, by contrast, the philosophy and symbolism of Zen Buddhism seems to have been so compatible with the freedom to design for immediate visual enjoyment, that visual and symbolic objectives were one and the same thing.

Even when a building is clearly designed to be seen, its appearance may require interpretation according to an invisible scheme of ideas. Photographs of some Hindu temples impress me as very deceptive in this way. The picturesque massing – 'jello-mould' piles or ornamental knobs and writhing statues – immediately suggests an arresting and agreeable abandon. The serious purpose can be appreciated only after one has studied an underlying symbolism that governs the ritual of ground preparation and establishes an arrangement of squares on the ground plane in which each area represents a divine or cosmic power.[7] It is the arrangement of plan squares, projected upward, that orders the pinnacles and determines the personages portrayed on the exterior; and it is the religious significance of these areas that causes the designer to disregard as irrelevant the natural properties of the stones that he raises upon them.

In Western architecture, the long survival and the repeated revival of a few neoplatonic conceptions provides the clearest illustration of the complicated connection between the objectives that may lead an architect to use a proportional system, and the expression that the system may be given in building designs. Superficially, a few conceptions may be said to have governed the pro-

[7] Stella Kramrisch, *The Hindu Temple*, Calcutta, 1946.

portional systems of the Middle Ages and the Renaissance. Both medieval and renaissance architects believed firmly in the Pythagorian conception 'all is number'.[8] The universe was thought to have a basic mathematical order, in which the elements of fire, earth, water, etc. were represented by geometrical shapes. This scheme, described in Plato's *Timaeus*, was developed by the neoplatonists, and had the sanction of a long line of theologians beginning with St. Augustine. Another conception, within the framework of the broader conception of the universe, was the identification of certain regular geometrical shapes with the perfectibility of man, hence, man made in God's image, and thence, man as a microcosm of the macrocosm. This chain of ideas had its foundation in Plato's *Meno* in which Socrates, by asking questions, causes a slave to make a diagram doubling the area of a square, and in this way demonstrates that 'learning is but remembering of our eternal soul'. The parallel between this demonstration and the geometrical 'secrets' that medieval masons had to know to

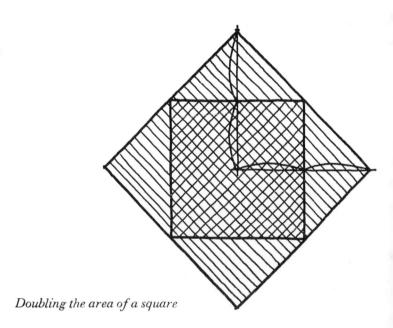

Doubling the area of a square

[8] Rudolph Wittkower, *The Architectural Principles in the Age of Humanism*, London, 1952 (New York, 1965), pp. 24-27.

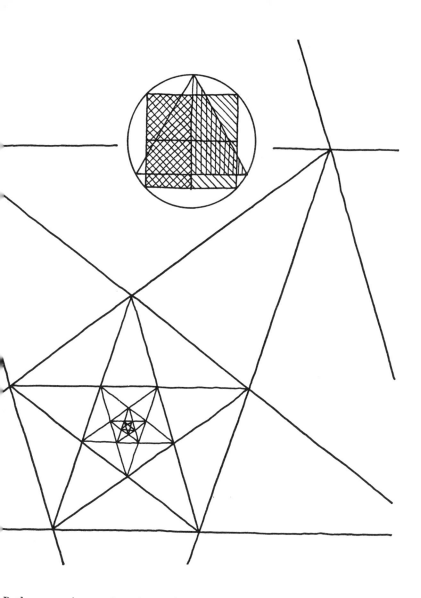

Both conceptions endowed certain shapes with near-sacred meaning

raise large buildings from small plans, was inescapable; and the shapes that lent themselves to this kind of a geometrical evolution from one shape to another acquired a symbolic meaning in addition to their practical value. Both conceptions – that of a universe of number and that of a geometrical order which, seen in the large, is an image of Divine Order and, seen in the small, is the image of man's path toward the Divine – endowed certain shapes with near-sacred meaning: the square, the circle, the double square, the equilateral triangle and its half triangle, the pentagon and the star formed by extending the arms of the regular pentagon. The geometry on which a building was based attained such a religious significance that in the Renaissance it was believed that 'if a church has been built in accordance with essential mathematical harmonies, we react instinctively; an inner sense tells us, without rational analysis, that we perceive an image of the vital force behind all matter – God Himself . . . it follows that perfect geometry is essential in buildings even if accurate ratios are hardly manifest to the eye.'[9]

What is remarkable, when we look for a systematic connection between these conceptions and the buildings designed under their influence, is the fact that the same beliefs and essentially the same ratios and geometries *could* underlie architectures as different as those of the early and late Middle Ages and the early and late Renaissance. And when we look for the reasons underlying these very different uses of geometry and measure, they are found in ideas only indirectly related to geometry. The principal change between the medieval and renaissance uses has been attributed to the changing conception of the Godhead: 'Christ as the essence of perfection and harmony having superseded Him who suffered on the cross for humanity; the Pantocrator replaced the Man of Sorrows.'[10] Another reason is found in important shifts in attitude toward antiquity, which maintained enormous prestige throughout these periods. In the Middle Ages the sense and science of history was hardly present, and classical precedent exerted a largely theoretical influence through descriptions and theological interpretations. Early in the Reniassance the architects began avidly to measure and record Roman ruins. From Alberti to Palladio they make it clear that their credentials are based as much on first hand acquaintance with the monuments of antiquity as upon a knowledge of geometrical systems supposed to be those of the

[9] Ibid. p. 25.   [10] Ibid. p. 27.

ancients. There was not, as yet, any serious conflict between Roman architecture, as measured, and the neoplatonic conception of numbers as it was understood.

It was the beginning of systematic archaeology, and the growing collection of precise descriptions of Roman (and later Greek) buildings, which delivered the death blow to the long evolution. It became increasingly clear that neither the ratios nor the geometries consistently fitted the accumulated evidence. And the final attempts to reconcile the two may be observed in the academic books of orders, where the finest antique entablatures and columns are shown measured by impractically minute modules, and by intervals that are arbitrarily applied to the shapes.

This evolution makes it clear that even where essentially the same ratios and geometries are used by the architects – maintained in this instance by a continuing belief in the religious and scientific significance of numbers – they may find expression in designs based on different, or even contradictory, orders of shape and relationship. And we may observe that this peculiar history is not unusual. Equally confusing relationships between a designer's reasons for using proportional systems and the shapes and relationships of his designs are to be found in Chinese, Hindu or Islamic architecture. We can only conclude that although – in the abstract – a tightly knit practical synthesis of a building calls for some kind of an equally precise order of visual divisions, by and large, the intentions that actually have led architects to use proportional systems are as complicated and as varied as the civilizations that they come from. It is only through the discovery of some common denominator of the systems used, rather than by a classification of the reasons for their invention, that proportional systems can profitably be examined as an ingredient of architectural scale.

A key is furnished by P. H. Scholfield in *The Theory of Proportion in Architecture*.[11] He shows that proportional systems may be analysed as mathematical and geometrical systems; and indicates that although the intentions of the designers are quite varied, very few basic systems are used. Looked at in this way, the different proportional systems are more or less perfect approximations of a few basic geometrical approaches; and each of them may be regarded as a more or less successful search for the system that will

---

[11] Peter Hugh Scholfield, *The Theory of Proportion in Architecture*, Cambridge, 1958.

yield the greatest number of similar shapes, similarly related. Scholfield believes that there are substantial reasons for this underlying regularity: that it tends to provide a set of beautiful relationships. Let us make use of the key that he supplies – the few regular patterns that the systems that have been used fall into – but let us reserve judgment as to whether they produce beautiful relationships or make some other contribution to design.

The module is the simplest and also the most limited proportional system, as it offers only the multiplication and repetition of a shape. These traits are conspicuous in Frank Lloyd Wright's 'honeycomb' houses, designed on a hexagonal grid. An idea of the difficulties of planning with this shape may be gathered from the occurrence of triangular closets, odd bathtubs, and awkward corners, even under the hand of a master. In plan, the wig-wag walls reveal that these modules do not combine to make larger simple shapes. The strength of the hexagonal module lies in the fact that it may be clearly read inside and out, and runs through the building in a way that is visually unmistakable. The roof shapes have been used to bind the hexagonal units into larger wholes.

The Japanese system,[12] using a six foot column and beam module and its sub-division into two mat areas, obviously is more suitable for practical planning, as these units will combine to produce a variety of rectangular shapes. However, the rectangular module, unlike the hexagon, tends to provide a less and less emphatic measure for the eye as the units are repeated in increasing numbers. The essential system is an infinitely extendible 'jungle-gym', in which the larger units of the design – whole building blocks and wings – tend to lose identity with the module that generated them. In Japan, this tendency is overcome by the magnificent crowning roofs that repeat similar shapes at sizes appropriate to the pavilions they cover. Because of this, it would not be inaccurate to say that two systems are actually used – one a module of repeated dimensions, and the other a large shape repeated at varying sizes.

Both Wright and the Japanese used large bold roof shapes to counter the visual monotony that results from merely parking modules side by side and to draw attention to the larger sections of the building. But a simple modular system also lacks relate-

---

[12] Arthur Drexler, *The Architecture of Japan*, New York, 1955. Werner Blaser, *Japanese Temples and Tea Houses*, Basle, 1956: see photographs and large clear plans.

divisions that are *smaller* than the module. In the Japanese house the mat unit, with its three foot and six foot dimensions, provides two useful small dimensions. But divisions even smaller than these escape the system's regularity. Wright brings his small details into harmony by a free play of shapes that are outside the hexagonal system, though they are often visually suggestive of it.

The improvisations that make these modular systems successful have not always been considered satisfactory. From ancient times, there have been architects who sought to discover systems of divisions that would provide the regularity of a module and, in addition, yield a graduated series of related smaller and larger divisions. A step in this direction is taken when, instead of a module, the divisions of the design are thought of as fractions of its whole extent: the important dimensions, for example, may be $\frac{1}{2}$, $\frac{1}{3}$, $\frac{1}{4}$ and $\frac{1}{5}$ of the building's length. The same method of division may be applied to any of these fractions of the entire length. For instance, the $\frac{1}{4}$ length unit may itself be divided by 2, 3, 4 and 5. In this way, an infinitely small series of divisions is found, fractionally related to the largest dimension of the building. Consequently, the architect has at his disposal a graduated scale of divisions in which the smaller sub-divisions are related to the parts in the same way that the larger parts are related to the whole length of the building. This appears to be the solution suggested by Vitruvius, who shows the sub-parts of a temple's column and entablature divided in this fashion. In describing it, he used the analogy of the human figure – remarking that in such a system the parts of the building are related to the whole as the parts of the body are related to its height. And this analogy, interpreted in various ways, has caused endless confusion through the years.

To be effective, this system must be judiciously adjusted to each particular design. For while an infinite number of fractional divisions may be derived from the total length, it is obvious that, as the variety of divisions is increased, it becomes increasingly difficult to relate them by eye to the whole length of the building, in the one case, and to the fractional unit that they subdivide in the other. Practically, the system can be used; but only by roughly laying out a building and then, by trial and error, discovering the fractional divisions that make their mathematical relationships clear to the eye. To those who pin their hopes on proportional systems, it poses a question. What other kind of clear relationship can be established between the fractional divisions, in addition to their common property of neatly dividing the whole length of the building?

An answer is found in the rejection of those fractions that are not sub-multiples of the whole length. When this is done, each division is not only related to the whole length – as a fraction of it – but it is assured of a series of fairly simple relationships to the other fractions used. For instance, in a building 72 ft long, the following numbers are available as sub-multiples of 72:

$$1 \quad 2 \quad 4 \quad 8$$

$$3 \quad 6 \quad 12 \quad 24$$

$$9 \quad 18 \quad 36 \quad 72$$

Other numbers, such as 7, 10 or 15, have been rejected because they cannot be evenly divided into 72; and those that remain are related in what is called a secondary harmonic progression ('harmonic' referring to mathematics, not to music). The architect has at his disposal units of 72 ft, of course, and the fractions:

$$\frac{1}{72} \quad \frac{1}{36} \quad \frac{1}{18} \quad \frac{1}{9}$$

$$\frac{1}{24} \quad \frac{1}{12} \quad \frac{1}{6} \quad \frac{1}{3}$$

$$\frac{1}{8} \quad \frac{1}{4} \quad \frac{1}{2}$$

To secure a related series of small divisions (as before) the 72 in division ($\frac{1}{12}$) could be similarly divided within the same scheme of relationships.

I hope that I have made it clear that this system, which falls into mathematical symmetry, fulfills the practical specification that a system of divisions extend to both large and small sizes, and that it develop a consistent set of relationships that are sufficiently simple to be at least partially understood by a spectator. It is probably the complete proportional system that Vitruvius was trying to describe; and it is the type of system that (imperfectly understood and carried out) was used in the Renaissance by Alberti, Brunelleschi and Palladio. It may be described in many ways, and it may use different sets of dimensions with varying degrees of ease. But we may notice that it is essentially analytical and commeasurable, and that it is based upon scales of preferred dimensions – fractions of a whole – that are linked in patterns of proportional relationships.

An inherent difficulty with 'harmonic' systems is the fact that because they are based on simple fractions of a whole dimension, the number of divisions available to a designer will be limited by the base number (or fraction) that is chosen. A system based upon the series $\frac{1}{2}$, $\frac{1}{3}$, $\frac{1}{6}$, for example, yields a much greater variety of simply related intervals than one based on $\frac{1}{5}$, $\frac{1}{7}$, $\frac{1}{35}$, etc. Of the great wealth of progressions that are mathematically possible, only a few realistically may be used for a particular building's design. In practice, the system usually has been applied only to some of the shapes of a design – for example, to the over-all building block, to the window and door openings, and to the columns and entablature of the order. When the architect carries the application further and uses it to control thousands of small details, he is likely to find the proportional system more a strait-jacket than a help in designing. 'Harmonic' systems provide the designer with the means to relate systematically large and small dimensions, to each other, and to the whole building. But they carry with them a very limited choice of clearly desirable dimensions.

Other systems based upon geometry tend to have the complementary advantages and disadvantages – a wide choice of divisions and difficulties in applying them to designing. The best known is derived from the 'golden section', and has recently attracted attention as the basis of Le Corbusier's 'Modulor'. The approach is different. Instead of providing the means to divide a given large dimension into fractions, it provides a system of intervals that are consistently related to each other. This is made possible by the unusual properties of a number $\frac{1-\sqrt{5}}{2}$, or 1·618. The ratio of one to this number, which is sometimes indicated by the symbol ϕ, may be expressed by a rectangle with a short and a long side. It makes possible the geometrical progression of golden section ratios: 1, ϕ, ϕ^2, ϕ^3, ϕ^4, etc., in which each number is the sum of the two preceding numbers, and related to the preceding number in extreme and mean ratio. The evenly related intervals, from the largest needed to the smallest, are automatically provided, without the device of fractions of one of the fractions that is used in 'harmonic' progressions. In geometry, the use of these ratios allows the greatest possible number of similar shapes to be constructed from the fewest different dimensions. This can be illustrated by a square ϕ^2 by ϕ^2, made up of rectangles and squares whose sides are 1 and ϕ. This figure has three different shapes, nine figures can be found in it, and it uses only the two

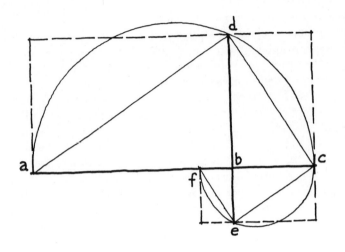

Extreme and mean ratios: $\dfrac{bd}{ab} = \dfrac{bc}{bd} = \dfrac{be}{bc} = \dfrac{fb}{be}$

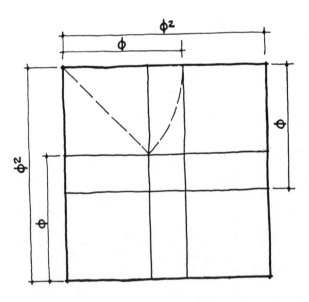

This figure has three different shapes, nine figures can be found it, and uses only two dimensions: ϕ and ϕ^2

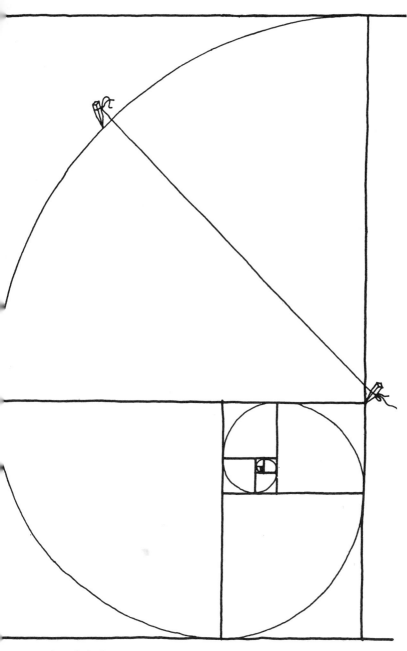

A series of similar rectangles, similarly related, generated to an infinite largeness or smallness

dimensions ϕ and ϕ^2. Another diagram, the 'whirling square', shows graphically how a series of similar rectangles, similarly related, can be generated to infinite smallness or largeness; and it also shows how such a geometrical series can be easily laid out with a compass, or a string and peg, in lieu of calculations. The richness of divisions that is yielded by the golden section is amply illustrated in Le Corbusier's *Modulor* 1,[13] There is nothing magical about this sequence, the numbers simply have their characteristic behaviour as a system of numbers. This particular one is picked for its behaviour as a ratio system and as a number sequence. Another series using the number $2 \cdot 414$, or $1 + \sqrt{2}$, may be as useful, while others have built-in advantages for various different tasks. But the mathematical properties of $\dfrac{1 - \sqrt{5}}{2}$ and $1 + \sqrt{2}$, as applied in geometrical figures, reveal an amazing economy of shape and an equally remarkable flexibility of sizes that appears to leave them without serious rivals. The difficulties lie in the practical application of this type of system to buildings that must be designed to scale and constructed to measurement. Most of the versatility that can be demonstrated on paper, in fact, has yet to be applied to architecture.

Le Corbusier, in his *Modulor*,[14] has attempted to solve the practical problems in several ways. He has used two golden section sequences to make a graduated scale that can be used by designers and builders alike. He has found a series of dimensions that allow fairly equivalent dimensions in feet or meters. And he has proposed that all component parts of buildings should be manufactured to the Modulor scale dimensions. His Modulor, however, has as its largest unit the height supposed to represent a man with raised arm (7 ft 5 in.), and provides sub-units suitable for a low or a high seat, for an arm rest, for counter height, etc. Thus the system 'measures' large dimensions in modules supposedly tied to 'human' dimensions; and, incidentally, it may be considered the most recent tribute to Vitruvius' analogy of the human figure. After examining the magnificent turbine release of dimensions by the number system of the golden section, this application may seem a little disappointing. I believe that it has another significance that we shall examine later.

The 'harmonic' systems that we have discussed provide a way

[13] Le Corbusier (C. E. Jeanneret Gris), *The Modulor*, Cambridge, Mass., 1954, pp. 89-99.   [14] Ibid.

to achieve a series of dimensions that are related to each other and to a largest size. The golden section not only allows this, but provides the maximum number of similarly related shapes at different sizes, and a mathematical and geometrical neatness that is almost unique. Nevertheless, each system has a fairly high purchase price. With the harmonic system the base number of the series must be carefully chosen to yield all of the divisions needed. The fractional parts, different for each building, must be translated into feet and inches, which they will not normally fit neatly. The golden section is even more awkward in that its intervals are not factors. The only practical solution is the manufacture of measuring sticks for the drafting table and for field work. In recommending these systems the architect has always believed that they tended to produce relationships that are in harmony with nature, or inherently beautiful; and this is the essential reason why he has been willing to bend his method to their capabilities rather than see, in each design, an order of shapes that is visually rewarding and suits the practical layout and construction. To evaluate their contribution to architectural scale, we cannot avoid asking if this kind of regularity is, in fact, beautiful and if it takes into account the subjective nature of perception.

Historically, the beauty of harmonic ratios, and the belief in the natural harmony of numbers, was given its most substantial support by the analogy to musical harmonies; and in the Middle Ages and the Renaissance it is the simple chord ratios $1, \frac{1}{2}, \frac{1}{3}, \frac{2}{3}, \frac{3}{4}$, etc., that were preferred in architectural designs. This support was demolished when the physics of sound showed that there is no true analogy between the relationships of dimensions as they are seen and audible chords. More fundamentally, the Pythagorean cosmology of numbers, which to be used even in the Middle Ages had to undergo 'conversion to Christianity' and in the Renaissance had to be filtered through another conception of Christianity and another philosophy, cannot possibly be revised to fit the post-Einsteinian world. It is the very expectation that an absolute universal order exists to be grasped which has been challenged. The possibility of equating geometry and number with magical or religious significance would seem to have disappeared for once and for all. The magic has not gone out of mathematics, which continues to spin new and wonderful works of relationship. But mathematics and the natural sciences have progressed to the point where they may clearly be seen as exercises in human imagination which – while they may hope to discover a 'unified law' for today – hold out no hope of finding a grand scheme for all times and for all places.

We cannot dismiss proportional systems because they may no longer be respectably held to represent natural or divine laws. Le Corbusier, who is one of the most inventive living architects, and who is often a brilliant analyst as well, holds that the shapes of the golden section are those for which the good architect is consciously or unconsciously looking.[15] From another architect, full of vague and quaint notions, this statement would sound suspiciously like a warmed over version of Socrates' 'remembering of our eternal soul'. But Le Corbusier is entirely in tune with the times, and thoroughly modern in his outlook. He makes it clear that his first search was for a system that would fulfil a very contemporary need for a unified system of shapes; practically, so that mass production would be harnessed to the benefit of building; and aesthetically, to provide the visual world of architecture, our cities in particular, with a badly needed antidote to visual chaos.

Nor can we dismiss the conclusions of P. H. Scholfield, whose mathematical analysis we have followed. He is fully cognizant of the transitory reasons that have supported the use of proportional systems at different times, and he is fully aware that the beauty of any isolated shape is a very dubious quality in the visual world of relative shapes and hues. It is the kind of relationship that provides similar shapes at different sizes that he believes to be inherently beautiful. Indeed, he appears to see no alternative to such a system except 'romantic intuitive' approaches to designing. Both Le Corbusier and Scholfield look to mature proportional systems to supply unity, which is conceived to be necessary to beauty.

I do not wish to become involved in the fancy game of aesthetic speculation, but if the words beauty and unity are not given some special meaning – as they often are in aesthetic studies – they stand for qualities of a work of art that neither spring from, nor are they developed from, a special category of shapes and colours within a design, nor even from a special category of relationships within a composition. Both of them are developed in, and depend on, all of the ingredients and relationships of a composition – everything that is associated within the work. The modes of

[15] This conviction resembles Viollet-le-Duc's argument that the equilateral triangle fully satisfies the eye; see 'Neuvième Entretien', *Entretiens Sur l'Architecture*, Paris, 1863. A comparison of Le Corbusier's and Viollet-le-Duc's discussions of proportional systems is everywhere interesting.

Beauty may emerge . . .

beauty and the modes of unity are as varied as the works of art
are. Beauty may emerge with spare and austere forms, sometimes
with frightening ones, as in some African sculpture or Egyptian
temples; or she may recline voluptuously in a design that tickles
all of the centres of sensation, as in the paintings of Tiepolo or in
the great tiled mosques of Isfahan. Unity appears in equally
varied forms. It may be Euclid-clear, as in the Parthenon or the
paintings of Piero della Francesca; or it may be organically com-
pounded in the most elusive ways, as it is at the Katsura Villa, or
in the paintings of Klee. Clearly, unless one wished to stand
champion for one of the particular modes of beauty that was developed in the past, or for a particular conception of unity – such
as Aristotle's in his ubiquitous conceptions of magnitude, order
and unity[16] – beauty and unity can only be discussed intelligently
as very general comprehensive qualities, or as they have been
created in a specific whole composition.

Even when it is possible to specify the quality of beauty, or the
kind of unity, that a proportional system is intended to promote
in a design, the extent to which it is seen and experienced depends
on all of the other shapes and colours seen with those of the
system. As early as the seventeenth century Perrault, the doctor-
architect of the Louvre Colonnade, questioned the validity of the
analogy between music and architectural proportions, and asserted

[16] Aristotle, *Poetics* IV.

. . . tickles all of the centres of sensation

that what is seen would govern the usefulness of the system.[17]
Lord Kames[18] noted that the relationships of proportional systems
are seen while the spectator walks about a room or down a street;
and that this movement, with the distortions of perspective that
accompany it, render the supposed exactitudes suspect. The shapes
of a proportional system are modified not only by perspective, but
by the complex interdependence of things seen at the same time.
Simple visual experiments show that all of the shapes, thicknesses, colours and values of light and dark outside the system
affect our experience of the proportioned shapes, and may even
prevent their recognition. Thus, an entablature and supporting
columns may be designed, in every detail, according to a system

[17] Claude Perrault, *Ordannance des Cing Espèces de Colonnes*, Paris, 1683.
Translated by John James as *A Treatise of the Five Orders of Columns in
Architecture*, London, 1708, p. IV.
[18] Henry Home, Lord Kames, *Elements of Criticism*, London, 1824, pp.
427–30.

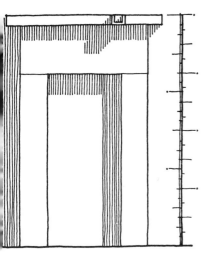

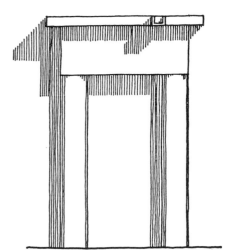

*Designed in every detail accord-
ing to a system of proportions*

*The ratios of column shape and
the shape of the space between
columns are strikingly altered*

of proportions; but the visual impression may be dominated by
effects that the system does not control. When round columns are
substituted for square ones, the ratios of column shape, and the
shape of the space between columns, are strikingly altered. In the
bright sun, shade and shadows dominate one's impressions; and
they do not coincide with the shapes set by the system. The low
sun may make long raking shadows, and dark shade on one side
of the rounded shapes. When the sun is overhead, the same
shapes may be given long beards of shadow, while the shade is
chased to both sides of the rounded shapes. These alterations due
to colour, texture, and shadow are the liveliness of architecture,
and only a lifeless diagram is free of them. Even in extremely
diagrammatic buildings – those of Mussolini's University City,
for example – the blackness of the openings and the whiteness of
the walls modify the shapes. One need not be dedicated to a
romantic, or a merely intuitive, approach to designing to worry
about the reality of the regulating lines. Is the geometrical order
of the system what is seen? We must recognize that proportional
systems are part of the larger order of all that is seen; and that if

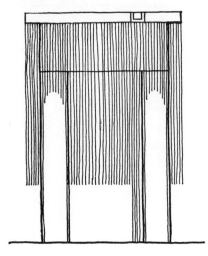

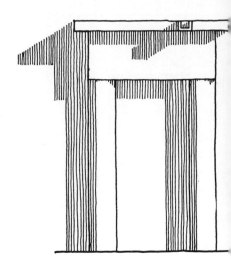

Long beards of shadow, while the shade is chased to both sides of the rounded shapes

The low sun may make long, raking shadows and dark shade on one side of the rounded shape

they contribute to beauty or to unity they do so because the designer is seeking to express, throughout the design, feelings compatible with their system.

The notion that there is an exact interval of relationship that – when put in a design and seen – evokes experience of beauty, is directly at odds with what we know about the process of seeing, with modern criticism, and with modern aesthetics. Can it be that what is consistently beautiful about these systems is geometrical and mathematical conformation in the abstract – beautiful ideas rather than beautiful building parts? If this is true, their use may be recommended, as other theories of creation may be recommended, if they enable a particular designer to make finer works of art. But the fact that many architects have sought unity and beauty through the use of these systems is not as good a recommendation as it might appear on first acquaintance. The history of taste makes it quite clear that these qualities have been different things to different people at different times.

Leaving beauty and unity alone, let us observe that visual proportion systems are valuable in architecture because they generate two kinds of order. They place an order of dimensions and relationships in the design which (when it is seen) may be used to control whatever the designer wishes to express in his design; and they place in the mind of the designer an order of divisions and relationships which, we shall see, can be a much needed stimulus to his imagination.

Calculation and Imagination

If beauty, or unity for beauty, are qualities peculiar to each generation and even to each composition, they cannot be accepted as the underlying purpose of proportional systems and we must look further. The systems that we examined in the last chapter showed themselves to be attempts to reduce the dimensions of a building to mathematical order. If these regularities are not merely traces of archaic beliefs in the intrinsic power of numbers, they must correspond to some architectural quality that the architect wished to secure for his design. To establish, in each case, a correspondence between the proportional system and what the architect seems to be interested in controlling in his designs, requires a scholarly enterprise that is well beyond my capacities, and hardly central to a discussion of architectural scale. But even an inconclusive survey is instructive.

The exact designing method of Greek architects has not been reconstructed. But the striking formal clarity and the precise execution of their temples has always suggested, to the modern eye, that a refined system of shapes must have been used. The most convincing attempts to discover the geometry that they employed suggest that it was of a practical as well as an aesthetic value. Thus Jay Hambidge, in his discussion of the Parthenon proportions,[19] supposes that the temple was laid out on a set of rectangles that have the practical advantages of congruence – for example, a golden section rectangle (1 to 1·618) plus a rectangle 1 to ·618 equals the $\sqrt{5}$ rectangle (1 to 2·236), which is constructed with peg and string, used as a compass, or by folding a cord to equal fractions of a whole dimension. And by means of a few of these shapes, the principal column centres, wall lines, and heights

[19] Jay Hambidge, *The Parthenon and Other Greek Temples, Their Dynamic Symmetry*, Yale, 1924.

could be laid out accurately and proportionately in the field from a small schematic diagram. The system of shapes allows ample small divisions, which may be generated in the same way as the larger divisions; and the details of the cornice or columns – which were governed by their traditional shapes – could be studied and refined within the same system of proportional rectangles. In this way, all of the divisions of the building could be related to each other, and to the whole length, width, and height of the building.

Greek inscriptions concerning architecture seem to indicate that much of the ingenuity that is spent in attempting to find an elaborate system of measurements may be misplaced. We may attribute to the ancient Greeks an anxiety to regulate all the relationships within a design that they did not have, and did not need, in an eminently traditional architecture. And we may fail to credit the Greeks with a skill in the logistics of construction which they did possess. In his explanation of the oddities of the Propylea of the Periclean Acropolis, J. A. Bundgaard provides a most convincing reconstruction of the way the architect Mnesicles may have worked.[20] He emphasizes the traditional nature of Greek

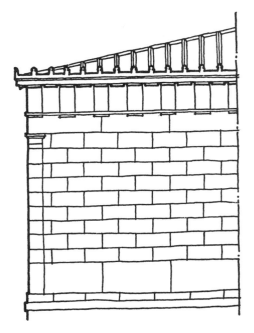

The main features of the design were almost automatically set

[20] J. A. Bundgaard, *Mnesicles*, Copenhagen, 1957.

designs, which were always modifications of previous buildings – often on the same site – and he describes a mode of construction in which the architect needed only to envisage his design as a general scheme, and could refine and correct it under construction.

From his general scheme, the architect described the building in terms of ashlar blocks and special members that were well understood by everyone connected with the building's erection. This specification served to control the quarrying of the stone and its rough dressing. The same system – of courses for heights, and block units for lengths – could be precisely established on the building when the base courses, of carefully fitted and polished marble blocks, were laid in place. The precise divisions may have been marked by a cord that was folded into equal divisions, chalked, and snapped to the wall. From these block-length divisions, the column spacings and the triglyph and metope divisions could be established; the vertical dimensions could be set from the stone courses in a similar fashion. Thus although the architect, no doubt, gave the greatest attention to the main regulating proportions as to both heights and widths – deciding how to modify the traditional shapes – the main features of the design were almost automatically set once the number and size of the building stones had been specified. The moulding of the shapes, and the refinements for the eye, could be worked out on the building during its translation from the rough blocks of the design description to a building of finished and polished marble units.

Whether one accepts Hambidge's or Bundgaard's reconstruction, the character of the proportional system is unmistakable: it brings the intervals of the design into relationship with the height, length and breadth of the building, and it does not extend beyond it. To the eye, what is striking is the casual treatment of the open spaces between temples – which appear to be governed by traditional sites rather than by what is seen – and the fact that the interiors do not seem to have been designed with a skill in any way comparable to that employed on the exterior design. There is also a peculiar failure to see some of the design continuities that are obvious to us. The west and east porticos of the Propylea, for instance, back into each other in a joint that can be best described as a collision; and it is not unusual for several buildings standing in a row, for example the 'treasuries' at Delphi, to be in different scales and serenely unaware of each other. Greek temples evince a strong drive toward the unity of solid shapes, as does all Greek art. But they show no interest in the control of relationships between solids that are not traditionally treated as a part of a simple block.

What is of special interest to us is the fact that the system used in designing seems to have had just the same limitations, and exactly the same scope, as the architect's conception of the whole design. The contrast that, to our eyes, exists between the extreme refinement of what is controlled and what, in fact, the architect is interested in controlling, is paralleled by the contrast between his system for relating the parts of the design to the building's length, width and height, and his apparent lack of curiosity about other relationships.

The nature of medieval proportional systems was concisely indicated by Paul Frankl.[21] A system of geometry was needed in order

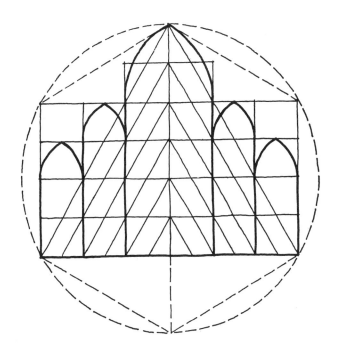

Heights could be raised from the plan dimensions, level by level

[21] Paul Frankl, 'The Secret of the Medieval Masons'; with 'An Explanation of Stornalocca's Formula', by Erwin Panofsky, *Art Bulletin*, Vol. xxvii, pp. 46–64.

to raise a building accurately from a small diagram, without the use of graduated scales. The problem was solved by the mason's training in the use of a number of geometrical key figures, the secret lore of his craft. By recognizing the key figures of a plan diagram he could develop the required shapes with only the sketchiest indication of the elevations. One of the key figures has come down to us. It illustrates the method for erecting a pinnacle based on plan squares. Each square is one half the area of the one below it, and is derived by setting a square diagonally within a larger square. This, you will recognize, is an application of the 'trick' described in the *Meno* which Socrates used to illustrate the nature of learning and knowledge. Another, different, example of the medieval use of geometry has come down to us through the records of a controversy concerning the completion of Milan cathedral. The argument was about the kind of triangle to be used in establishing the building's height. The triangles – in this case, either an equilateral or an isosceles triangle – were used to build a scaffold of measurements. The widths of the plan were used as triangle bases and, by means of modular rods, the diagonal sides of the triangles were crossed to establish the major heights. In this way, the heights could be raised from the plan dimensions, level by level, as the building was constructed; yet the diagram of the whole could be controlled accurately.

Thus, we may assume that medieval churches were planned according to simple geometrical grids that established the vaulting bays and the major heights. And we may suppose that the larger masses -- for example, the buttresses and pinnacles – were generated from the plan shapes by systematic geometrical keys understood by the masons. Smaller details, such as moulding shapes, were either left to the mason or controlled by wooden patterns furnished by the architect. The eye informs us, regardless of the exact proportional system, that the Gothic was developed from the Romanesque on the matrix of a linear diagram of ribs and belt courses. The tying system of geometry preceded the imaginative control of the design. The evolution of control, over the years, indicates that the architect was first trying to shape the interior into a coherent set of relationships, then extended his attention to the gabled façades and towers, and that he was only able to control the entire ensemble of the exterior in the last brilliant hours of the flamboyant or perpendicular Gothic. Regularly, when a medieval building was effectively pulled together, the unifying touches were added late. As in classical Greek architecture, the schematic diagram may be said to have preceded a sure imaginative grasp of the whole. In the rapidly evolving medieval church architecture, the educational gesture of including the chevet and transept ends in one sweep of an arc, or of using a grid of equilateral triangles to set the heights from the plan, may have been a necessary prelude to the architect's comprehension of the relationships before his eyes.

The proportional systems of the Renaissance may be discussed with some assurance, as a number of the architects have left us writings on architecture as well as their buildings. The period is dominated by the analogy of architectural proportions to musical intervals – supported by the neo-platonic belief in the power of numbers that was discussed in the preceding chapter. The resulting proportional systems were largely the ratios generated by simple harmonic progressions of numbers, and they were applied to whole façades, room shapes, and even to the entire design of buildings. For the designs are now thoroughly drawn up before construction, and controlled by the architect in every detail. The most comprehensive scope of application may be found late, in the work of Palladio who conceived of suites of rooms in which lengths, widths, and heights were in harmonic relationship.

What strikes the eye is the renaissance struggle to conceive of buildings as a whole – a continuation of the medieval problem, with the added problems of a sculptural approach and antiquarianism – and the limited success that they had. In the villas of Palladio, both the measure of control and its limitations are interesting. All of the major rooms and the façades of the building may be governed by the proportional system; and the order may extend into the garden through long wings, terraces and walls, resembling those of an ancient Roman villa. The serene confidence with which all that is in view has been brought into visual order is impressive. But it is obvious that Palladio did not care to integrate the parts of his design beyond a certain point. The rooms, harmoniously related in over-all shape, remain separate chambers, each with its scheme of decoration and connected to the others through narrow doors. The façades remain separate compositions of a plane, as well as satisfactory faces of the building block: and the buildings extend into the landscape only tentatively. If the proportional system applies to all of the major shapes, it nevertheless stops well short of controlling a three dimensional spatial system. Even in his most freely composed 'Mannerist' buildings, Palladio's eye demanded a clarity of definition, and a simplicity of relationship between parts, which is not inherent in the proportional system – although it may reflect common sense in avoiding an over-complicated use of it. This simplicity resides in the architect's imagined conception of the design, and it is in fact one of the main traits of character that makes these buildings unmistakably Palladian – noble, poised and serene.

Whenever it is possible to compare a proportional system to the control of shapes that an architect commands in his design, a similar connection is suggested. Proportional systems are used by the architects as a matrix, to solidify and extend their imaginative grasp of the relationships to be controlled. The mathematical ratios and geometrical figures are useful only when they are accompanied by a vivid imaginative grasp of the part of the design to which they are applied. In some instances, the part of the system that cannot be imagined, or does not interest the designer, remains unused – and this seems to be true of Palladio's use of harmonic ratios. In other instances, as in the development of the medieval church, it seems highly probable that the architect's control of successively more complicated wholes could not have been developed without the stimulus of the proportional system's 'machine' for generating relationships. When proportional systems are regarded in this way, it is easy to see why the Baroque architects relegated their use to routine regulation, while their designs rapidly moved to control all of the interior and the out-of-doors as grand suites of interpenetrating spaces, where views – similar to theatrical scenes – govern much of the design. The beginning of this shift of interest has been observed in Palladio's

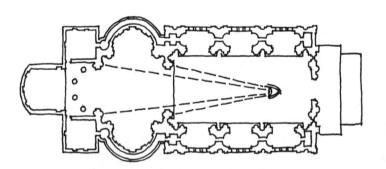

The beginning of this shift of interest

56

Redentore Church, where the nave and chancel are unified by repeated elements – the one framing the other with the 'effect of a stage setting.'[22] The transfer of interest, from the abstract regulating shapes to the visible aspect of the building as it appears in light and shade, must be charged to the architect's sure imagination of a visual world that needs no clarifying diagram. Certainly, it is not owing to a lack of interest in geometry or regulating systems. The Baroque architects were the supreme masters of the complex shape, and this was the very age of dogma and hierarchical order. Looking backward in time, one is tempted to see in Hellenistic architecture, and in the Flamboyant and Perpendicular Gothic, similar relegations of proportional systems to the routine. The designers were pushing the rest of the design forward to explore a well established visual world. They intimately knew how each view of each new arrangement of the design would be seen by a spectator.

With this kind of a connection between systems and designs, the modern re-emergence of interest in proportional systems is not surprising. Viollet-le-Duc's publication of his observations on medieval proportional systems[23] was the first great stimulus to a renewed interest. And it was influential precisely because it accompanied his rational theory of the connection between design and construction. Not only was the Baroque vein of imagination worked out, but the creative vision of the post-Baroque architect was not able to cope simultaneously with the appearance and the physical facts of machine-age engineering. Proportional systems as well as modular structural conceptions were taken from the storage closet and put to use again. And it is, in part, the problem of co-ordinating prefabricated units and materials that has sustained our interest in proportional systems and led Le Corbusier into the middle of aesthetic proportional theory. But another problem, having directly to do with the scope of imagination, has been equally responsible. The perceptive modern architect has an understanding of the scope of relationships that must be controlled in visual design, that has far outdistanced his imaginative creation of designs to control them.

The contrast is striking. For all their positive accomplishments, modern architects do not show in their designs the sure imaginative control of relationships throughout a building, to the lands-

---

[22] Wittkower, op. cit.   [23] Viollet-le-Duc, op. cit.

cape, and to the townscape, that was common in the seventeenth or eighteenth centuries. Yet we have a much more highly developed understanding of these same relationships than ever existed before. The superior understanding is simply a continuation of the control of relationships evolved in the works of Palladio and of the Baroque architects. It is developed to a more comprehensive scope, and – by a jump in imagination – we are able to conceive of defined space as a continuum. Le Corbusier calls this 'ineffable space'. Like most important ideas, once it is understood it seems very simple. 'Once you have grasped the notion of space as a fullness – as a plenum of something – you will also see, I am sure, the inevitable corollary that space is naturally and patently a *continuous* whole, reaching out in all directions from any given point to far beyond the largest community of men. . . .'[24]

Gestures toward the conquest of this expanded domain have been many times remarked upon. At times they have been obvious, as in the flowing space of Wright's open interiors, or in his extension of the building's module to the yard. They have even been made diagrammatically clear. In Mies' Barcelona Pavilion, details of the design that might not illustrate the conception of a spatial continuum seem to have been deliberately swept away – making the building a textbook illustration. But the mode of conception also leaves its mark where designs are sculptural, and the continuum of space is not made their primary reason for being. It shows in the fenestration of Wright's closed-shape Johnson office building; and it inhabits the joints between the swelling forms of the Ronchamp chapel – where a ribbon of light has been introduced between wall and roof, and the line between the exterior and the interior moves so that it is sometimes well outside the building's enclosure and sometimes well inside of it. What we are attempting to control is not just the block (Greek) or an interior and block (Medieval) or a Palladian suite of rooms and façades, but the Baroque world of all that is seen indoors and out. And the modern architect's understanding of this entirety goes a step further to grasp what, at present, appears to be the ultimate scope. He begins the design with the assumption that he is dividing off a continuous defined space, and that it is seen by a moving observer, whose way of seeing must be accommodated.

This enlarged conception of the ensemble is the background to

[24] Norman T. Newton, *An Approach to Design*, Cambridge, Mass., 1951, p. 85.

Le Corbusier's Modulor. He begins with the thought that space should be measured as sound is measured in music (not at all the Renaissance analogy between architecture and music); and he assumes that the ratios that the Modulor generates are the ones that an architect will normally choose if he is afforded the opportunity to do so. The modulor scale is to be used as a tool in the imagining of real buildings, in real space, and at actual size. And he even goes so far as to say that he will violate the system whenever it interferes with free imaginative conception. Whatever the limitations of the system that he has invented, he is certainly seeking a proportional system appropriate to the widest conception of the relationships that can be controlled in designing. In terms of this essay, he is looking for an armature to help the imagination to conceive of, and to order, the most complete set of relationships that architects have ever attempted to synthesize. This includes surface, mass, and defined space. It extends indoors, outdoors, and to the inter-relation between them. It includes whatever is seen, not as a congruent entity, but as part of a continuum that can be opened, divided, closed, and fragmented at will.

This elaborate speculation on the connection between proportional systems and the scope of architectural design may seem to have strayed from the subject of architectural scale. The later portions of this book will show that it is very much to the point. But for the present, let us observe that it suggests that a useful proportional system of shapes, or a useful system of shapes to control scale, must at least be compatible with the complex relationships of the space continuum as they are seen by an observer. Informed architectural opinion would support this assertion, in any case; but there is an additional reason that is not tied to current theories of creation. This breadth of conception is a comprehensive one that includes the more restricted conceptions of the past. In the construction of a cumulative understanding of scale, nothing less will do.

Human Scale

Up to now, the human being who looks at a building has entered our discussions of scale as a somewhat disrupting afterthought. After describing the order of dimensions that naturally grows out of practical designing, it was necessary to remark that this regularity is not always apparent to an observer. After examining some of the reasons for proportional systems, it was necessary to ask if their harmonies are always seen by an observer. It is when we turn our attention to human scale that we find the spectator himself supplying the point of departure; and we should not be distracted from this beginning by other uses of the term 'human scale'. The role of the human in human scale has been carelessly assigned, for example, to the imprint of man's theoretical six foot height throughout a design – a rather inhuman use of his image. It has been sentimentally assigned through equating small scale with 'the humane' – a view which surprisingly ranks Marie Antoinette, for her Hamlet, more humane than Thomas Jefferson for his Virginia State Capitol or, compounding the confusion, makes her a superior humanist. These absurdities and other common mistakes, we shall see, are the results of developing sweeping maxims from small bases in fact. In the mature conception of human scale, the central premise is the fact that size and relationships of sizes, as the spectator experiences them, are 'illusion':[25] that there is no simple correspondence between dimension size, as it can be measured on a building, and the spectator's impression of size. If this is true, the way in which he arrives at his impressions of size must be the controlling factor of visual scale.

Everything that has been established about human perception supports this assumption; and the reasons for it are apparent in

[25] See Gropius' discussion of reality and illusion, op. cit.

Superior Humanist

Less Humane

the simplest, most basic activities of seeing.[26] When light strikes
a surface, a portion of it may be reflected into the spectator's eyes,
where it stimulates light-sensitive rods and cones that may be
compared to photo-electric cells. This energy is then transmitted
to the brain through the nervous system. The intensity of the
light that is reflected furnishes the basis for our perception of
values of light and dark; and the wave length of the light furnishes the basis for our perception of colours. The boundaries
between these qualities furnish the basis for our perception of
shapes. But it is only when the cues sent by the nervous system
have been matched to appropriate figures of the visual memory
that seeing – in the normal sense of the word – has been accomplished. Thus, the image is stimulated by what lies before the
eyes; but it is not at all an automatic impression. Even the simplest acts of perception involve a complicated matching of visual
stimuli to a lifetime's store of remembered experience. All of this
is accomplished so quickly that the spectator is hardly conscious
of the activity. Actually, he has painfully acquired the skill in
childhood and has been developing it ever since.

[26] James J. Gibson. *The Perception of the Visual World*, Boston, 1950. Ida
Mann and Antoinette Pirie, *The Science of Seeing*, Harmondsworth, Middlesex,
1950.

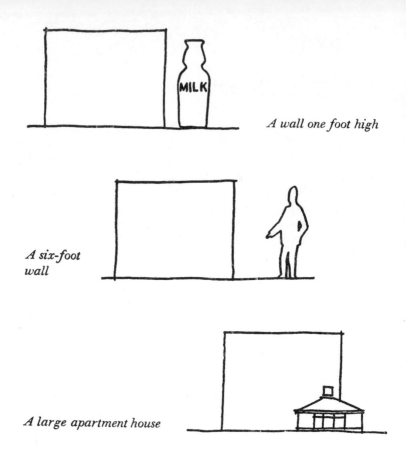

A wall one foot high

A six-foot wall

A large apartment house

In such an activity, there obviously can be no absolute qualities of colour and shape, of light and dark, or of size; for each of them must be influenced by other colours, values, or sizes, seen at the same time. Many of the familiar optical illusion diagrams show this clearly.[27] A grey spot, surrounded by green, looks pink; surrounded by red, it takes on a greenish cast. Two straight lines are the same length by measurement; but the one with outsweeping Y ends appears longer than the one with inturning arrow ends. The same rectangular figure is interpreted variously as a wall one foot high when a milk bottle is next to it, as a six foot wall when a man is standing near it, or as a large building dwarfing a small

[27] Lavishly illustrated in Gyorgy Kepes, *The Language of Vision*, Chicago, 1944.

house. Applied to architectural scale, this relativity of impressions means that the apparent size of a division, or of a shape, in a building is affected by the other divisions and size relationships in the same view. And it indicates further that the shapes that have customary recognizable sizes may be counted on to 'measure' the architectural elements seen with them, and to assume a particular importance in the perception of sizes. Thus, when the spectator looks at one wall of a room it may be assumed that his impressions of its height are influenced by its width, its surface texture, and even the pictures hung on it. But the recognizable size of a chair standing before it indicates a special definite measure of the surface.

Perception involves much more than the organization of a view, of course. Efficient use of the eyes requires them to be constantly on the move. Only a small central area of the retina of each eye has the maximum sensitivity needed to stimulate the clearest images. A band around these centres is less sensitive; and the peripheral borders stimulate only shadowy impressions. In addition, the eyes cannot focus on near and far distances at the same time, nor can they pick out small details with the greatest clarity and at the same time embrace a wide field. To sample adequately what is spread before them, they must be employed in constant motion and change of focus. Hundreds of views – some focused, others spread wide, some near, others distant – are needed to supply the basis for a clear visual impression even of a small room. To see a whole building, literally thousands of views must be organized before it is visually experienced in the most superficial way.

A spectator is neither wiping the design with eyes that record the surfaces, nor is he separately organizing single images. Normally he joins the interpretation of one view to the next, to the next, to the next, in uninterrupted series; and the way that he sees a building very much depends upon the ease with which his impressions of size, in each view, can be carried on to the next view. Superficially, it determines whether perception will be sufficiently pleasant to encourage his looking at all. More profoundly, it determines the depth of meaning that the experience may have for him. A room in which he must radically revise his impressions of size with each view would be a nightmare. If it were possible to construct one that successfully frustrated the observer's every attempt to relate his impressions of size, it would no doubt make him actively ill. A crowded junk shop, where there is little sense that can be carried from view to view, is difficult to take in. The spectator who is compelled to see every part of it clearly – as he might be in searching for some valuable article – will probably have a headache. By contrast, in normally pleasant surroundings, architectural or natural, the impressions of size in each view are compatible with, and developed from, those formed in the preceding views. Because they indicate a continuing standard of size, they help rather than hinder the complex task of organizing visual cues.

But the eyes are much more than de luxe optional equipment of the mind and body. Ease of perception opens the windows through which the intellect and emotions may respond to the environment; and the continuity or discontinuity of the observer's impressions of sizes determines the depth of meaning that architecture can have for him, as well as the rapidity and ease with which he perceives it. In fine architecture, where the relationships between sizes are precisely planned to be seen, the spectator is freed from concern about relative smallness or largeness and encouraged to enter into visual experience with an intensity that is not otherwise possible.

At this point, it can be seen that an analysis of the observer's perception of sizes and size relationships may easily become lost in

he thickets of subjective experience. Fortunately, the comments
hat have been made will suffice for our purposes: Size is a rela-
ive rather than an absolute quality of visual experience. Shapes
with customary recognizable sizes may be counted on to 'measure'
he other shapes seen with them. The spectator must be able to
arry a standard size, from view to view, for clear and easy per-
eption. With these facts in mind, we may examine the factors of
human scale. And we may begin with the shapes, with customary
ecognizable sizes, which are encountered throughout a building,
nd may be expected to indicate a consistent standard of size
wherever they are seen.

People themselves provide the most dependable categories.
buildings usually have people in and around them; and we are so
amiliar with our own genus that a human figure that is excep-
onally short, or tall, or immature, is quickly recognized for what
: is. Because of this, the human figure must be thought of as a
ind of measuring rod that, at any time, may appear with the
arts of a building, applying a standard size to them. But even
when the observer is alone and sees no people, the height of his
yes from the ground, the perspective angles of his views, and his
ocusing for distances, enable him to judge sizes and distances
elative to his own size and position. Thus, a small room will be
measured' for the spectator by the people standing and walking
bout in it, by the relatively flat angle at which the ceiling is
een, and by the exclusively near focus of his eyes. In a large
oom the people would appear relatively small, the ceiling would

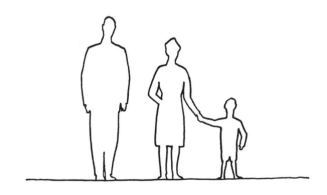

Tall, short or immature

65

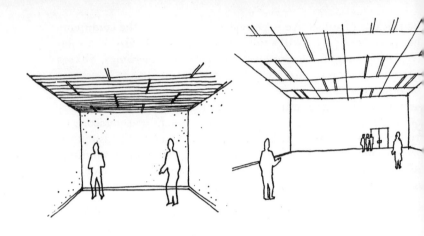

be seen at more acute perspective angles, and the spectator woul
use a focusing for distances that was not needed in the smalle
room.

Human size also leaves its imprint on all of the parts of a buil
ing that are designed to be intimately used by people. Stairs, fc
example, may have riser heights as low as four inches, or as hig
as eight; but they must be designed to fit the human stride. Cor
sequently – whether they have a low riser and broad tread, (
high riser and narrow tread – they provide a fairly reliable indic
tion of size that can be recognized when it is seen. Railings als
normally vary within height limitations that make them a reliab.
tip-off to size. Cabinets, counters, shelves, door knobs, light swi
ches, and to some extent widow sash and doors, take their dimer

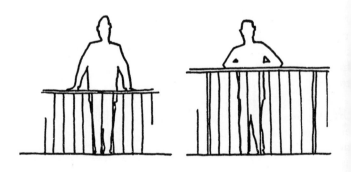

Railings normally vary within height limitations

66

To reach the top shelf

To work without stooping

Toe space

ions from bodily positions that have been found convenient and comfortable. The very similar dimensions that are used for them over and over again in architectural designs carry with them an imprint of size recognized by the observer. But in the architectural interior it is furniture that most consistently carries a standard of human size. A chair may be designed for erect posture,

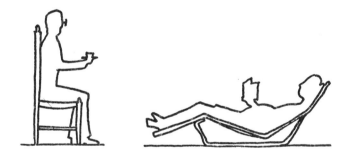

r for lounging almost on the floor; but if it is to be comfortable, it must accommodate the body in these positions, to the inch, or to the fraction of an inch. Its size is widely recognized and understood wherever it appears.

All in all, the human figure is a unique module of architecture the common measure of the ensemble.'[28] Where people are seen in or near a building, where the parts of the building that they touch and reach are seen, and where the spectator carries his

[28] Georges Gromort, *Essai sur la Théorie de l'Architecture*, Paris, 1946, 111.

personal estimate of sizes and distances relative to himself, a uniform standard of measure is introduced into architecture.

Where there is no imprint of the human figure, the order of physical scale which we have discussed may often be understood by the spectator. We are trained by a lifetime's experience to recognize many of the customary sizes of building materials that may have originated in convenient dimensions for manufacture or for construction. We found that the size of a brick, for instance, probably originates from convenience both in firing and in brick-laying; and has, in the U.S., been further refined to fit the four inch modular standard. Where it is seen it implants a measure of the other shapes that are seen with it. The strips of a sheet-metal roof are a convenient width for manufacture on rollers, and for spacing the standing seams that accommodate the metal's rapid expansion and contraction with temperature changes. The resulting striped pattern of seams indicates a size that measures the roof and the distance of the spectator from it.

In a more complicated fashion, structural logic supplies relationships that may indicate size and distance to the observer. Where the way of building is simple and familiar, the spectator will recognize the manner in which the loads are distributed and how they are carried to the ground; and his eye will quickly grasp the effort occasioned by long spans and by loads piled high above

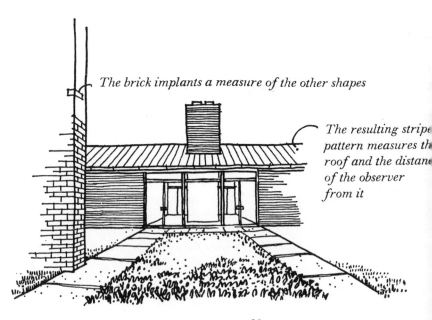

The brick implants a measure of the other shapes

The resulting stripe pattern measures the roof and the distance of the observer from it

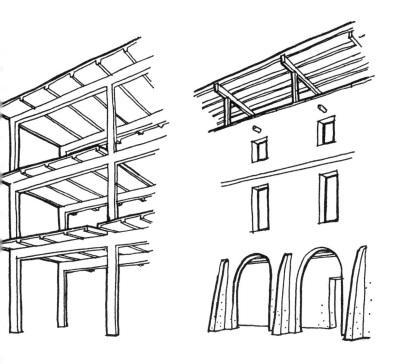

Where the way of building is simple and familiar

he ground. The width of a supporting column, the depth of a
beam, and the apparent load supported, may instantly imply that
a span is large or small, without expert knowledge. In a more
general way, life on this planet has made the spectator aware of
some of the structural consequences of the immutable pull of
gravity. Without conscious rationalization, he recognizes that in
large buildings, as in large animals, the structure must be relatively heavy, while miniature structures like the spider may re-

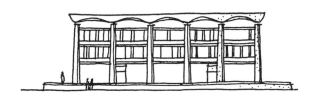

In large buildings, as in large animals

The structure must be relatively heavy

quire proportionately much lighter construction. In these way
the building itself, its materials, and its construction, furnish
many sizes that are fixed by custom and recognizable; and many
which, if they do not precisely measure the other parts of the
building, nevertheless are indicative of a consistent measure of its
size.

A simple description of the idea of human scale has to do solely
with the spectator's impressions of the size of a building, relative
to his own size and position, and relative to these shapes with
customary recognizable sizes. A building is in human scale when
it is designed so that the human figure and other objects with
recognizable size look normal in it and against it. People seen close
up or at a distance do not look surprisingly large or small. Perspective angles and focusing for distance do not surprise. Familiar
materials and arrangements of construction appear, in the building, neither larger nor smaller than expected. In the context of
the design, stairs, automobiles, and trees, are as big or as small as
you expect them to be. When this is accomplished the spectator
may perceive the building without being surprised by any of its
sizes; and the standard established by his first views will greatly
facilitate his interpretation of view after view, throughout the
building.

What is accomplished should not be underestimated. By elimi-

70

nating surprising sizes, this simplest version of human scale meets a prime condition of clear perception. The observer is relieved from concern about sizes, and fully freed to participate intellectually and emotionally in the design. Moreover, the architect has made it possible for the spectator to examine the building as a part of his world of reality. When the observer can assume that sizes are what they appear to be, he is able unquestioningly to accept his direct experience of the design; and this has an important effect on the nature of the experience that he can derive from it. I suppose that everyone has, at some time, been led around a great building or monument while a guide rattled off the information that it is so many hundred feet high, so many thousands of feet long, and that it would contain all of the people in Kansas City if they were packed into it. And I am sure that everyone has

So many hundred feet high, so many thousands of feet long, it would . . .

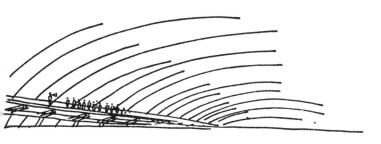

Contain all of the people in Kansas City

71

found that, under the circumstances, it is difficult really to perceive the design. The information about the size of the building, and the speculation about it, makes it almost impossible to experience directly and vividly. In a similar manner, a building that cannot be perceived according to an assured 'real' standard of size conjures up the question of its size and of its reality. Direct experience is muted and sensations are blunted, as they filter through the haze of indecision.

It is what may be called a clinical observation of the building, as opposed to the uninhibited experiencing of it. And in human scale, as it has been described here, the spectator's experience is not allowed to become clinical. He is free to explore architecture as another unquestioned reality in his real world.

For all of its virtues, we cannot rest contented with this simple description of human scale. It is an oversimplification that glosses over the problems actually encountered in designing. It conveniently establishes a negative criterion that can be paraphrased in a sentence: the building fits the spectator's mode of perception when it is designed so that there are no surprising sizes. But like the excellent negative criteria for design in general, 'nothing needs to be added, nothing can be taken away', it presents problems of technique and of scope. How do you do it? Is this all that you should attempt to accomplish?

We should immediately notice that, as a measuring rod, the human figure presents serious problems of technique. It functions well only when it is *made* to measure effectively. Our judgment as to how large a person should look, and our estimate of size and distances relative to ourselves, tends to be excellent when the person, and what is measured, are close to us. In the absence of other means to gauge sizes, it becomes rather unreliable in a moderately large room or before a modestly large building; and it is extremely unreliable for long distances, for large rooms, and for big buildings. Skill at estimating people's sizes, and at quickly calculating personal relationship to the surroundings, appears to be largely developed in ordinary work and play, where the urgency diminishes as people and objects become further and further removed from personal contact. Naturally, architects, and some other specialists, develop unusual skills in judging distances and sizes, from the nature of their work. I have had several class exercises, intended to develop these skills in architectural students completely upset by the uncanny judgment of field artillery

72

Window glass has increased in size

cadets. But the judgment of sizes and distances by the ordinary spectator of architecture must be expected to become more and more unreliable as they are removed from his immediate surroundings. Because of this, both the human measuring rod and the spectator's judgment of sizes relative to his own size and position, are fully effective only when the architect finds a way to extend their influence from near the spectator to far from him, and from the parts of a building to its whole extremity.

We must also notice that although the recognizable sizes of building materials and the sizes implied by structural arrangements help us to judge the size of buildings, they are most reliable when they have been frozen by custom to set dimensions and relationships of size. Throughout history, conventional sizes have played an important part in architectural scale; but in our time of rapid change they are apt to be a frail measure. The size of window glass, for example, was a very effective small unit of measure for long periods when it was kept to approximately the same maximum size by the techniques of glass manufacture. With advancing technology, window glass has increased in size to the point where each year brings a new world's largest pane of window glass, and we are not surprised to see it at any size.

73

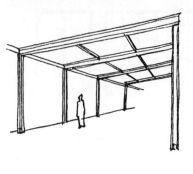
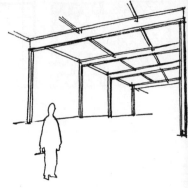

*A steel beam to span fifteen feet
is not strikingly dissimilar to one
that spans forty feet*

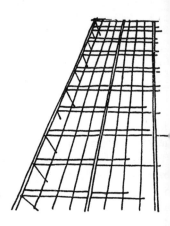

*Their diminution toward the top
of a large building may be hardly
discernible*

    The same advance has flooded the market with building materials that have sizes which are not generally or widely recognized; and it has made possible structural systems that are so efficient as to be impassive, showing their size in very minute changes of dimension and arrangement. A steel beam to span fifteen feet is not strikingly dissimilar to one that spans forty feet. Steel columns may be even more impassive. Their diminution toward the top of a tall building may be hardly discernible. This must be contrasted with the ease with which the structural efforts of other materials may be read. The difference in stone arches of fifteen and forty feet would be quite obvious. A stone lintel of forty feet, if it could be found at all, might have to be designed so deep as to crack under its own weight. When masonry columns are superimposed

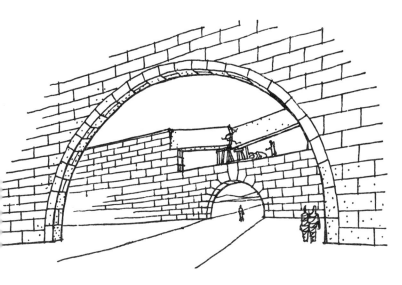

The difference in stone arches would be quite obvious

for several floors, the effort clearly shows in their thicknesses, and often makes the lower floors very cluttered indeed.

But even where the building materials are familiar, their use may be less than clear to the eye. Ordinary bricks, stood on edge in cavity wall construction, result in shapes that are of little help in measuring other shapes. Indeed, the familiarity that makes the brick shape, and other customary shapes, helpful in judging the

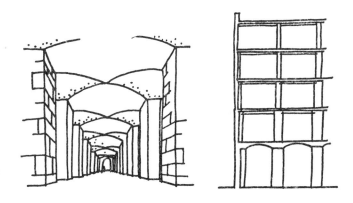

Makes the lower floors very cluttered indeed

size of a building, also constitutes a trap where they are repeated at altered size. In using a cavity wall, with its unusual high bricks, or in using a new material, the architect takes great care that the other shapes of the design firmly state a standard of size, and the unfamiliar shapes do not 'measure' erratically. To do this, and to direct the sizes implied by those shapes that infer something about size, but do it rather indecisively, he must find a way to bind all of the shapes that have implications of size into a system that firmly states a single standard of largeness and smallness.

In large buildings a system of relationships of size that spreads the influence of the human measuring rod and firmly establishes a measure of building parts is doubly necessary, because of the relative scarcity of shapes with recognizable size, and because of their generally small size. More often than not, when the architect goes about designing a large building, he discovers that shapes with recognizable sizes are not required in sufficient number to control the spectator's impressions – and this may be one reason for the useless balconies, stairs, benches, and planting boxes, that are sometimes introduced into buildings.

In a small room the furniture, plaster, boards and doors, may quickly convey a standard of size to all parts of the design. But these, and most of the more reliable cues to size, remain at very nearly the same sizes when they are parts of larger and larger rooms. In a spacious house they begin to be insufficient to give a rapid measure of the big rooms and long facades. In large buildings, and in the much larger exterior spaces around them, they may be so insignificant as to convey nothing at all at first glance. And when study makes them clear, they are likely to be difficult to relate to the largest dimensions of the design. Because of this, the larger the building or open space, the more of the problem of merely getting across a measure of the size automatically becomes difficult. The system of relationships of size that the architect has used to relate shapes with recognizable size to the larger divisions of the design is an important feature of nearly all large buildings that are skilfully designed.

As none of the measuring rods of customary or recognizable size can be considered entirely reliable, and as the most reliable standard (human size and shapes designed for human use) becomes increasingly ineffectual as the buildings increase in size, it is apparent that they cannot be casually spotted throughout a design. Human scale, as it has been defined here, requires a consistent standard of size throughout a design. It must be imple-

In large buildings they are likely to be difficult to relate to the biggest dimensions of the design

mented to be effective. The influence of reliable measuring shapes must be spread to the whole design through a system of part to part, part to whole, relationships. Shapes that have vague connotations of size, must be tied into a firm network of relationships that welds their tentative measures into a cumulative certainty. That this can be done is easily indicated.

In a room with piers that define an aisle on each side, the spectator will be close to one of the piers wherever he chooses to stand, and may conveniently gauge its size. The regular spacing of the piers makes it easy to judge the whole extent of the room – five bays long – and the beams that carry this spacing across the width of the room further distribute the measure. In his near

*The spectator will be close to one of the piers wherever he
chooses to stand*

views, the texture of the masonry and the block joints indicate a
standard of size which is easily attached to small areas of the wall
and to the piers. The whole shape of the room is immediately
linked to this intimate experiencing of size, by the big bay divisions. In the far views, the depth of the beams, and the thickness
of the columns, reinforce the first impressions.

Out of doors, a structural system may divide a whole building
into four quickly grasped parts. The size of these parts is measured
by the brick sizes, the size of the columns, flashing, etc. But the
end bay is treated to make this certain. It has a canopy at the
expected height, ordinary doors, and the door handle where it can

78

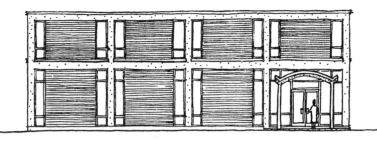

A ladder of sizes, each arranged within the other telescopically

be easily grasped. A ladder of sizes, each arranged within the other telescopically, measures first the structural bay and then the whole building. The control is, appropriately, most effective at the doorway where people approach the building and where the direct personal experience of its size, in relation to oneself, could be disrupting.

It should be obvious from these simple illustrations that the architect can adjust and regulate the ladder of sizes as he pleases, and that the way that he chooses to make a distribution system is intimately tied up with his approach to design and with the vocabulary he uses. But before we observe other types of distribution systems, let us return to another technical problem of human scale.

In the definition of human scale that we have begun to modify, the word normal is more complicated than it may seem to be. There is no reason to doubt that a building is in human scale when people, and shapes with recognizable sizes, appear normal within and near it. This is a limited conception of human scale, but a feasible one. But 'normal' cuts two ways here. There is the normal appearance of the human figure and familiar shapes – which we are well accustomed to recognize and need not question – and there is the normal appearance of their relationship to a building, which is a variable quality that must be explained.

A dramatic illustration of this variation is furnished an American traveller abroad who visits different cities in rapid succession. On first arriving in Rome, he is surprised by the apparent smallness of people and furniture in his hotel room, and by the relative largeness of the room's dimensions. On the streets he is impressed

Their doors, windows, and even their mouldings are surprisingly large

Tightly packed town of small alleys and little arches

by the general largeness of the buildings, although the city is without skyscrapers. Their doors, windows, and even their mouldings, are surprisingly large; so that against them the small European cars look even smaller than he expected. After a week's stay, he no longer notices this unusual relationship. It becomes normal. When our traveller arrives at Venice, this variable relationship contracts. In this tightly packed town of small alleys and little arches, people and furniture seem larger; and he will need a few days to become accustomed to feeling larger in his surroundings. If he then flies over to England – to rest from speaking Italian – a few days will be required before he becomes accustomed to a toylike Cotswold village: the rooms that lie about his feet when he stands up, the windows that he completely fills when he leans out of them, and the stone roofs that resemble those of a Christmas cookie house. Even this world, lived in for a while, can become normal for him; and he is likely to make another revision of his standard when he returns to America.

This trip indicates that in different places the spectator anticipates different normal relationships between people, or familiar

Windows that he completely fills

shapes, and their architectural background. The difference may be striking from country to country, where cultural, emotional, and practical forces have shaped very different customary relationships. The people who live in each country see with eyes trained by a lifetime's experience in the surroundings, and each relationship is normal in its place. But it is not necessary to go half way round the world to observe variations of this kind. In a less extreme form, they exist at home. Consider the surroundings of a young couple who live economically in a small apartment, and those of their parents who live very comfortably in a large house. Both places may be in human scale, so that people and furniture look normal against the walls. But when the parents want to give the young people some of their fine furniture, great diplomacy is needed. In the small apartment low slung chairs and coffee tables, small lamps and pictures hung below eye level look normal. When your host brings you a cup of coffee, he towers over your chair; and when guests get up to leave, the room seems suddenly crowded. All of this looks normal, partly because of the smallness of the rooms, but also because the circumstances of the young people make it seem appropriate and attractive. It is expected. In this context, the gift of a good-sized chest of drawers

The gift of a good-sized chest of drawers

Cheap, small and insubstantial

from the parents house may be as welcome as a hippopotamus in the bathtub.

A small room in the parents house – the morning room where the mother's desk and telephone sit – is the same size as the children's living room. But if the children are not very careful, the birthday-present lamp they have selected for this room (which was handsome in their living room) will appear cheap, small and insubstantial in the morning room. The chief reason for this may be the more substantial furnishings of this room and the larger rooms that surround it. But it is also a consequence of the way a spectator feels about, and thinks about, the furniture of an older couple in comfortable circumstances and of conventional habits.

Examples of this kind are endless in variety. The normal relationship between buildings and people, between buildings and familiar shapes, varies greatly from culture to culture. And within a culture it is susceptible to infinite gradations, corresponding to the meanings that we attach to our surroundings. Variations in the normal are expected between buildings that house public or communal institutions, as opposed to private ones, rich as opposed to poor, elegant as opposed to crude, male as opposed to female, exclusive as opposed to common, important as opposed to unimportant.

Variations in what is normal even derive from the actual materials and construction of architecture, because of the spectator's preconceptions concerning them. The spectator expects one normal relationship between himself, other people, or recognizable

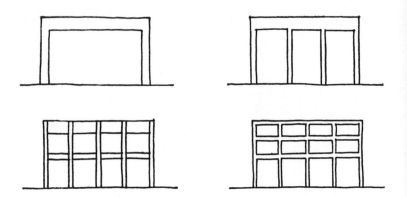

In the absence of other evidence, the more divisions that are used, the larger the building appears

A design with no units or divisions is enigmatic

The spectator's attention is led back to the block shape

sizes, and a masonry building with arched windows; and another between them and a frame building with guillotine windows. In the first instance, he will accept as normal quite a small feeling and relationship to the masonry construction; while the same relationship to the frame building will usually seem abnormally small. Still other relationships are expected with steel buildings sheathed in metal, with precast concrete structures, with a poured-in-place building, etc.

To the variations in the norm that are caused by building materials and construction, we must add the variations evoked by a bay system, or any other system of unit divisions that the building is given. These not only transfer the measure of the human figure and customary sizes to the whole building shape, but at the same time they influence the norm of relationship that the observer expects. The discovery of this fact may very well make a designer, working on his drawings, a little drunk with power. On paper, his diagrammatic alteration of these divisions seems to control completely a design's apparent size. In the absence of other evidence, the more divisions that are used, the larger the building appears. The observer expects a building with more units to be larger and one with fewer units to be smaller. The same effect is gained by the use of a smaller or a larger shape within the whole block – as when a roof or the windows are made smaller or larger. But at the extremes, a design with *no* units or divisions is enigmatic; and when the divisions are so numerous as to create an over-all pattern or texture, they may fail to suggest large size because the spectator's attention is led back to the block shape that the pattern fills out.

Without a doubt, the divisions themselves lead a spectator to expect different norms of size, without reference to the human figure or to shapes that have customary sizes. We shall see that this influence plays an important part in the architect's manipulation of the spectator's impressions of size. But the simple relationship between the divisions of a drawing and impressions of size is, of course, a paper illusion. In an actual building the architecture at some time will have to be seen with the human figure, and undergo close personal investigation. Where the norm suggested by the purely formal divisions of a building is contradicted by the human measuring rod, or by other cues to size, the element of surprise that is introduced may make human scale, as we have defined it, impossible. But the divisions may also be used to influence the observer just short of surprising him. And in accomplishing this, the influence of the divisions may be seen to have its own inherent symmetry in relation to tell-tale cues of size. When a large building is made to appear smaller, by the use of fewer divisions, the suggestion is easily accepted as an alteration of the normal relationship between a building and the human figure, etc. But when a small building is made to look smaller, the effect may quickly become surprising. Similarly, when a small building is made to look larger, by the use of more or smaller divisions, the effect may easily alter the observer's normal expectations. But when a large building is made to appear large, the effect quickly becomes surprising. Thus, where the norm suggested by a system of bays, or other divisions, is reasonably well supported by the observer's further experience of the building – the large building

*When a large building is made to appear smaller, the suggestion is
easily accepted as an alteration of the normal relationship*

*When it is made to appear larger the effect quickly
becomes surprising*

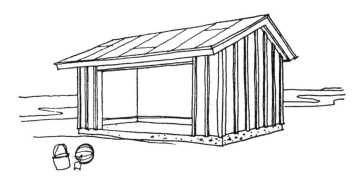

When a small building is made to look smaller the effect quickly becomes surprising

When a small building is made to look larger the effect may easily alter the observer's normal expectations

found to be larger than supposed, the small building smaller – its influence upon his expectations may be considerable. And where a group of buildings, or an interior, surrounds the observer, this variation of the normal may be substantial.

We have found that the normal appearance of a human figure, or of recognizable objects, with a building may vary considerably from country to country, where the surroundings – suggestive of one or another different normal relationship – have conditioned the whole population to expect it. Within a culture, what is normal varies in a more subtle fashion according to the use of the building, its status in the community, and the way that people think and feel about what it houses. And even building materials, ways of constructing with them, or the formal division system of the design, give rise to somewhat different expectations and consequent slight variations in what is considered normal.

Living within a homogeneous culture, the architect can sense these nuances with ease: his experiences are the same as everyone else's. It is when he ventures to design buildings outside the community that it becomes necessary for him to be fully aware of these variations in the norm, and to take them into account in his design. But I am afraid that there are other reasons to point them out. They have sometimes been overlooked because the architect designed his buildings as purely personal expressions, out of social context. More often, surprisingly, they have been overlooked because the architect followed a conviction that human scale means a single norm applied to everything everywhere – blindly ignoring the wide range of effects, from exactly right to startling, evoked by this inflexibility.

The normal appearance of human scale is real enough – as real as social attitudes and institutions. But it follows meaning, and it cannot be precisely fixed to a simple standard. To achieve a completely normal relationship between the spectator, the human figure, shapes with customary size and architecture, the designer continually changes the relationship. When its minute adjustments roughly match the preconceptions of the spectator, it is normal.

Human scale is based upon a fact that can be ignored only through the deliberate cultivation of a most peculiar naiveté. It takes into account the illusory nature of sizes and relationships of size, as they are experienced. It seems safe to assume that its point of view must be accommodated in any conception of architectural scale that is suited to our times. We shall see that its relationship to the ideas of physical scale, and to proportional systems, further supports its adoption as the basis for an understanding of architectural scale. Its simplest form, which we have summed up in the negative rule of no surprising impressions of size for the observer, may be made effective when it is revised in two important ways. First, in order to control a free observer's impressions of size, the human figure and shapes with customary or recognizable sizes, need to be co-ordinated into a system of easily related sizes. Secondly, the normal relationship between these 'measuring' shapes and a building is a variable that must be deduced by the designer from the surroundings in which he lives

88

and from the meanings that the people of his community attribute to their environment.

These amendments to our original description of human scale make it an idea that can be applied to the design of buildings. But a final important question about human scale remains to be answered. Does it, even in the amended form, encompass all that scale should contribute to architectural design?

Large and Small Scale, as Expected

The spectator's inconsistent expectation of different standards of size – in different places, for different uses, and on different occasions – should not be resented. It is a fair measure of his lively response to his surroundings and of their importance to him. If the people of Rome have a standard of largeness that is different from that of the people of Levittown, it is because their ideas, emotions and history are different, and because they are responding to their surroundings. If the spectator assumes that the judge will look a little smaller in the courtroom than he does in his dining-room, and even larger in the bathroom, it is because he has preconceptions and feelings about a man's relationship to his background – it has meaning for him. In architecture, this rapport between the spectator and his surroundings is often used, in reverse, to shape his experience. The standard of size is shifted to carry meanings that are recognized by the viewer; and these abnormal standards, large scale, small scale, and above all variations in scale, contribute an eloquence to architecture that can be obtained in no other way. If human scale does not allow them, it carries with it restrictions that have not been applied throughout the history of architecture. We shall see that this limitation is just what some architectural critics are prepared to assume. But for the present, let us assume that a useful description of scale allows for variations from the normal, and that the exclusive standard of human scale that has served as our point of departure is not always desirable. A second glance at the observer's problem of joining view to view will show that, under certain conditions, the eloquence of scale variations may be put to use without damaging the continuity of perception.

To be sure, the negative rule that no sizes shall surprise the observer has a firm basis in the activity of perception. Consistently maintained, it allows an observer the easiest and clearest vision and opens the window to his full participation in the experiencing of architecture. Where it is lacking, he must withdraw some of his energy from the enjoyment of architecture and apply it to mere comprehension or to clinical analysis of his own experiences. But we have already seen that the way in which a person expects to see people and familiar objects in relation to a building varies with the culture, the building, and even from room to room, according to his preconceptions and his past emotional experiences. Clearly, the mind that demands a certain continuity of size for perception is also a subtle calculating machine capable of simultaneously organizing impressions of size, ideas about size, and emotions relative to size. If departures from the norm of human scale – large scale, small scale, or variable scale – contribute valuable qualities to design (and they always have done so) they must not be discarded merely because they contradict the simplest possible description of human scale. Rather, we must discover the kind of design arrangement that allows a spectator to participate in variations from the scale norm while he retains the continuity of size impressions that is essential to significant experience. To do this, we must look further into the nature of his experience and, to begin with, distinguish between two aspects of it: variations from normal relationships of size through large or small scale, and variations in the continuity or discontinuity with which these standards are maintained.

The effect of large and small scale variations depends very much on the degree of their departure from the normal and upon the spectator's preconceptions. At one extreme, where the design only slightly departs from the normal and the deviation is expected, the spectator will ignore scale variations. People are accustomed, for example, to rooms furnished in a harmonious miscellany: Georgian desk, Danish-modern chairs, Japanese lamps, and that Victorian love-seat Aunt Matilda left me. It is not unusual for some of these pieces to be in a slightly larger scale than the others. A careful examination would reveal that a person looks a little smaller seated before the desk, larger in the new chairs, and small again in the love-seat. But the difference is slight; one expects such different-looking pieces to be different; and the variations in scale have no substantial effect upon the spectator. They would be noticed only if you passed into this room from one in which the most precise control of sizes and impressions of size had been exercised – one of those Louis XV rooms for which the furniture was especially designed, or a Mies interior in which

91

every chair had been placed within an eighth of an inch. We may assume that people are looking for a uniform standard of size or, more precisely, that they may be counted on to try and organize their views in the easiest way. Where it is possible, they will group near treatments into a rough standard that will serve as a convenient norm.

A spectator will also, without surprise, accept definitely large-scale treatments where he expects the qualities evoked by a large scale. I am not surprised, standing before the door of a church, to find that it is nine feet high and that I must reach up a little to grasp the door knob. I feel a little smaller in this doorway. It is a little impressive. It seems satisfactorily to announce the large room beyond and to represent the institution housed within. It has this effect, even at a distance, because the dimensions of shapes that have a customary size are a little larger than usual (panels, trim, knob height, and the door itself) and because the small details that might have been added to keep it in normal

I am not surprised to find the door is nine feet high

It impresses, but what is the meaning of it?

scale have been left out of the ladder of sizes, while the larger units have been emphasized. This difference in scale treatment attracts no attention, and it is accepted as normal. At the same time it provides a distinctive kind of experience. It makes me feel small, as seems appropriate here, and it makes the building seem impressive, which is equally appropriate. A similar variation in scale where it is not expected may attract attention to the unusual treatment of sizes and provoke an unfortunate clinical speculation. A recent fashion for 'impressive' front doors provides an example. The large-scale door, set in an ordinary house, is not expected; it attracts attention. I feel small in it. It impresses; but what is the meaning of it? Does my neighbour think that he is a baron?

You can now see that if the architect does no more than sensitively respond to what is expected, he may design in large scale, and derive the expressive values of impressiveness, etc., without surprising the spectator. And he may go even further so that his design not only accommodates but also heightens the observer's expectations. The church door may be made very large in scale so that it visibly gains in size as I approach it – making me definitely feel smaller – and so that it is very impressive indeed, approaching the awesome. The qualities are exaggerated; but as I am expecting a larger scale, the quite large scale clearly interprets for me what had been only an unconscious expectation. When I see the church and the neighbouring houses together, I am conscious of the difference in scale treatment. But the jump in the standard of size is one that I was predisposed to, and I am

*a 'real life' fact has been given extra emphasis and
clarity of meaning*

not likely to waste energy analysing what was done. Rather I feel
that a 'real life' fact has been given extra emphasis and clarity of
meaning. Obviously, if the same impressive scale were given my
neighbour's front door, the heightened experience would not be
accepted in the same way. I would not only suspect delusions of
grandeur but paranoia as well; for in this instance the gesture of
large scale is a bluff, without the meaning to back it up.

The use of an enlarged scale to meet expectations, and to
heighten and interpret them, requires sensibility in each instance;
and each case will be slightly different. Nevertheless, it is possible
to make some general observations. One of them is rather odd:
as a building becomes larger in actual size, people expect it to have
a somewhat larger scale. This is, perhaps, because it is difficult to
design the relationships of size in a very large building without
enlarging the scale. Large dimensions in the distributing ladder

94

of sizes are very badly needed, in order to measure the whole building shape, and they tend to dominate one's impressions, making the scale larger. Thus in Salem, Massachusetts, or in Williamsburg (towns where for whole blocks the scale is well controlled) you may see five houses in a row, two of them in a quite small scale, two in a larger scale, and one in a largest scale. The degree of variation is not great, but clearly observable, and it is accepted as appropriate to the size and pretensions of the house in each case, without causing the spectator consciously to revise his standard of size.

Where the degree of variation is great or unexpected, the spectator will be surprised. The Washington Monument is the extreme case. It is very large and in colossal scale. The only subdivisions that measure the over-all shape are the large stones, which are ineffective at a distance. It stands in a broad open mall, and it is given scale only by the trees and flagpoles near the base. It looks big at first glance, but as you approach it or study it you become increasingly aware of its size. The effect is a release of latent power attributed to the structure: powerful and awesome. It is also surprising, and there is a clinical ingredient in the experience. You are very likely to be concerned with its size, and with the difference that you find between its actual size and the original apparent size. In this instance the clinical question finds a satisfactory resolution in the over-all meaning of the design. The monument is understood as a tribute to George Washington, the first president; but it is also understood as a monument to the aspirations of the

in this case the gesture of large scale is a bluff

new republic of near continental size. Size, sheer size and greatness, are relevant to its message, and the power of the large scale is effective.

Where there is not such a proper place for clinical speculations in the meaning of the building, the interjection of the clinical awareness of size illusion is disastrous, and the surprise is freakish. Another national monument, the Statute of Liberty, is a borderline case. She certainly inspires affection, standing above the harbour and seen at a distance. But when you are near her, or peeking through her hair-do, it requires a most rigorous patriotism to abstain from speculating on her sheer size, and on the grotesque aspects of a woman this large. The case of some of our great public housing complexes is probably more relevant. The rows of huge blocks are impressive; and they tend to a very large scale when seen at a distance, because the budget has not permitted the architect to add the details that would measure the size from afar. The huge over-all shapes dominate. You may count the windows, but there is nothing in the design to help you to relate these very small spots to the bigger shapes. The impression is one of a growing awareness of size, latent power, awesome bigness, and a clinical concern for size. And because this message is inappropriate to the occasion, the effect is rude and depressing.

Largeness of scale – departing from the norm of what is expected – is a powerful expressive instrument that may be used to make designs eloquent. It is accomplished by making familiar objects larger than usual, by emphasizing the large units in the distribution system of sizes, and by leaving out or suppressing the small ones. While the way to produce the effect of large scale may be described as a mechanism, large-scale effects are typically unstable from design to design. The experience they afford can not be separated from the design's over-all meaning. The spectator's impressions of size, after all, are an inherent part of his whole experience.

A similar observation may be made of small-scale variations in the norm of scale. But the way they are produced and the characteristic experience that they afford is different. And for reasons that shall be clear, small scale has had a much less frequent use in architecture. The small, or residential, scale of architecture is, in fact, the 'human scale' that we first described. I find it at my house where – as I live modestly – the doors, cabinets, furniture, etc. set the standards of size pretty exactly, and the minimum spaces for human use establish many of the dimensions. The

You may count the windows

ystem for distributing sizes has little trouble in measuring the
over-all shape of the house, and there are ample details to complete the lower rungs of the ladder of sizes. The effect is soothing
to the ego. Returning bruised and tired from the office, it is
relaxing to discover that here everything is made to my measure.
It is what one expects of a small house. Applied to another building, the same scale treatment can be depressingly coy. I have in
mind those large country houses that, by small scale treatment,
seek to pass themselves off as cottages. The over-all shape that
accommodates 100 rooms can hardly be seen, as it is broken down
into small-house sized wings. These are given the same treatment
as my house; but the effect is precious. This is the danger of small-
scale treatment: its intimacy easily disintegrates into preciosity.
Where it is appropriate, small scale may be heightened to inter-

*Large blocks are much less emphatic than the smaller
units of measure*

pret a design with great effect. Some of the dormitories at Prince
ton are designed in this way. On first impression, they are domi
nated by the familiar neo-Gothic vocabulary – stone mullione
windows, arched doors, oriole bays, and high slate roofs wit
many chimneys. As you study them, they shrink a little. A ma
at a window pretty well fills it. You must enter through th
centre of some of the arched doors to find headroom. All of th
familiar vocabulary is a little small in actual size; and the larg
blocks have been so broken up with gables, chimneys, and win
dow groupings that they are much less effective than the smalle
units of measure. Full value for size is appreciated immediately
and that value is a little inflated. The effect is picturesque an
occasionally just a little affected. But it makes the student feel a
home; and it emphasizes the private and individual nature of hi
room, opening off the entry stairs, as opposed to the lecture hall
Consequently, it helps to carry out the educational aim of makin
each student feel an individual, rather than a cog in an education
machine. Certainly the scale is quite small for the kind of archi
tecture, but it does not surprise or cause one to speculate upo
size. The treatment of scale is similar to that of the large cottag
that we examined. But in its purpose as a residence for students i
finds a meaning – suited to the scale – which was not present i
the cottage for elderly adults.

As in the case of large scale, the heightening of an expecte
small-scale variation is a powerful expressive instrument that goe

wrong when it is not appropriately applied. But the dangers are even greater because a small-scale design, without appropriate meaning, is ineffectually pretentious. Consider the local bank vice-president's small adaptation of Mount Vernon, complete with portico and cupola – its size, at first glance, is bound to suffer deflation on further acquaintance. In the dormitory design there is perhaps a built-in element of affectionate contempt: one wants to pat it on the head as you would a child or dog. But for Mount-Vernon-in-miniature there can only be pity, or downright ridicule, as it has insufficient collateral to secure its borrowed pretentions.

The extreme case of small scale, which is so far from the normal as to surprise, is very tricky indeed. There are few architecture students, I imagine, who have not fallen in love at some time with an architectural model. The architectural vocabulary – usually seen at a formidable size – is reduced to a small fraction of the dimension. It flatters you subtly by the unexpected smallness of what it suggests; and the element of surprise is eliminated, because the model is understood as a replica. A children's playhouse may evoke a similar impression: cute, abnormally small, but not surprising. Clinical interest in size is evoked, but it finds

Cute, abnormally small, but not surprising

a place in an over-all meaning, because it is not inappropriate to the idea of a playhouse in which children play at house. The same small-scale effect is disastrous where there is no such meaning related to it. Consider the misuse of a concrete shell shape capable of spanning 100 feet. Your first impression is of a moderately large structure (a small version of this structural system) but when you enter it, you discover that it is very small indeed. The structural shape, with its intimations of size, has been used at an inappropriate size, and you find yourself surprised at its smallness. The effect can be ridiculous. I remember a church constructed on the economical 'A' frame which, across the lawn, looks to be a good-sized building and very impressive. As you approach, it shrinks; and as you enter, you can place the palm of your hand on the porch ceiling. It is appealing, but as a church its pretension are comical. The experience is all dénouement.

Large-scale and small-scale variations from the norm must be considered as expressive instruments for the designer. They contribute definite qualities which – in the context of different designs – have very different effects but remain within a roughly

You find yourself surprised at its smallness

100

predictable family of character. Small scale is achieved by making shapes with recognizable size, such as stairs, and those with connotations of size, such as structural systems, somewhat smaller than usual. Then the distribution system of sizes is designed to emphasize the smaller units, while the larger ones are made less emphatic. Its effects may be intimate, subtly flattering, soothing, precious, ridiculously toylike, etc. Large scale is achieved by increasing the size of shapes that have recognizable or customary sizes and by leaving out, or suppressing, the smaller units of the distribution system of shapes. Its effect may be grand, strong, or crude and clumsy.

As a rule these effects have two objects, the way they make the spectator feel about himself, and the qualities they cause him to attribute to the design. Thus, a small-scale design may make the observer feel a little more important than usual, and at the same time it may cause him to attribute friendly emotions to the building. Large-scale treatment may both cause the observer to feel somewhat removed from low egotism, and cause him to attribute more than human power to the structure. The expressive value of these effects has a powerful basis in the shifting of fundamental relationships between the observer and his environment. It is because of this that mistakes in scale, and accidental impressions of size, may be so shatteringly disturbing. And it is for this reason that interpretations of buildings by planned adjustments of scale – as compared to many other compositional arrangements – are inescapably effective.

We have observed that whether variation in scale surprises and shocks, or is accepted without hesitation, is a function of degree on the one hand, and of expectation on the other. Thus, the effect of relationships of sizes cannot be isolated from the observer's other intellectual and emotional experience of the same time. In fact, it is the cushion of coincidence between variations in scale and the other meanings in a design that normally allows an architect to employ the expressive values of large and small scale without introducing a sterilizingly clinical view of the experience. And it is those rare programmes in which surprise, or concern with sheer size, contribute to basic meaning that allow the freak distortions of very large scale and, less often, very small scale.

I am aware that this emphasis on the importance of experience that is not a direct response to formal arrangements will not please everyone. The appallingly literary tendencies of nineteenth-century criticism left most of us with the desire to study the

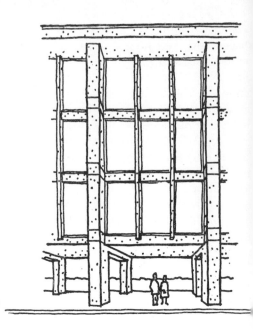

Some of the
relationships 'feel big'

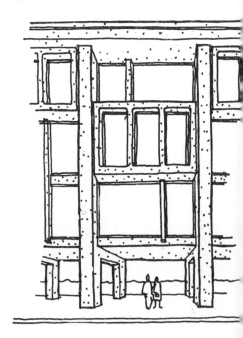

Elephantine

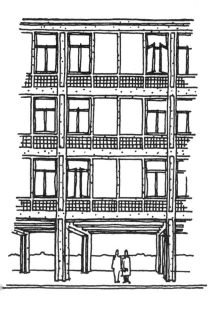

Tends to be fussy

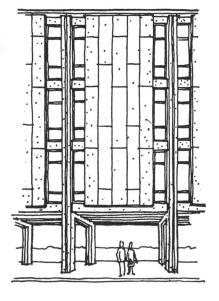

Nervous elegance or
waspish nerves

purely formal factors of design. But we are discussing the scale of architecture. And although it may be possible, by a great educational effort, to get people to look at paintings in a gallery as 'pure abstraction', it is impossible in architecture, where abstractions – constructed at great size – are immediately seen as part of a real not-at-all-abstract environment.

In one area in particular, emotional responses to what is perceived directly affect impressions of size. And the family of emotions that is involved is one that must be recognized before there is much hope of a designer's understanding how to control large, small, or normal scale. This is the response that Geoffrey Scott brilliantly isolated as 'feeling of bigness'.[29] The ordinary spectator of architecture has emotional responses of bigness and smallness that he cannot normally be expected to differentiate from his estimate of size. Scott cited the example of the Victoria and Albert Museum in London. Anyone can see that it is large, but no one would suppose that it 'feels' large; rather it is an awkward, fussy building. Most of us have experienced this confusion in regard to a friend or acquaintance. There are people whom we persistently remember as a big man or a big woman, although we have had their size repeatedly measured for us against the height of other people and we know that they are average, or even small in stature. There are Chinese vases and pots that, even when you place them on a table and tower over them, radiate a feeling of bigness that dominates you and the room.

This emotion is probably a consequence of symmetry, in the better sense of the word. The parts are so well related to each other, and to the whole shape, that the design acquires a sort of centripetal force of purpose. This makes its physical size less important in the experience that it affords than the relationship within the design. This emotion is an important ingredient of monumentality. And proportional systems have probably been used by architects to develop this quality, primarily, and only secondarily to 'measure' designs.

This emotional response and the observer's inability clearly to distinguish it from physical size considerably complicate the effect of scale variations. First of all, large-scale treatments tend to have a feeling of bigness. The big, bold divisions and the elimination of fuss that is used to establish a large scale, usually develops some of the symmetrical design relationships that 'feel big'. But when

[29] Geoffrey Scott, *The Architecture of Humanism*, Boston, 1914.

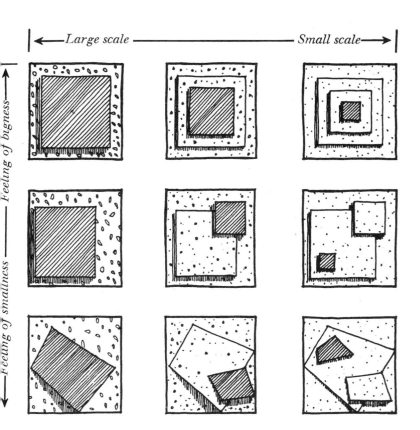

It shows the independence of large-small scale from feeling of big-ness-smallness and the affinities of large scale for bigness and of small scale for triviality

large-scale design is trivial and fussy, its large-scale effect of power is apt to seem clumsy and elephantine. Conversely, small-scale designs tend to be fussy because of their repression of the bolder divisions and multiplication of small elements. But when the architect provides feeling of bigness in a small-scale design, it acquires a fine elegance that is a very special character. The effect of this combination may be one of nervous elegance with wiry strength – like a spirited racehorse – or, alternately, one of was-pish neurotic nerves. What we must emphasize is the fact that the observer, in his quick estimate of size, cannot be expected to

105

distinguish feelings of bigness-smallness, or grandeur-triviality, from the effects of large and small scale. But the architect, in order to control his designs, must clearly understand how the effects of the building are produced. A useful exercise in developing this skill is a controlled visual comparison of designs which contrasts variations from great feelings of bigness to triviality with variations from large to small scale. It is probably impossible to execute it absolutely accurately, with all smallest-scale examples at exactly the same scale, and all maximum feeling of bigness examples just as big in feeling. But it shows both the independence of large-small scale from feeling of bigness-smallness, and at the same time it reveals the affinities of large scale for bigness, and of small scale for triviality.

The problem of disentangling feeling of bigness-smallness from large and small scale is a special one – because of the spectator's failure to distinguish between them. But it illustrates the inter-dependence between variations in scale and other qualities – that are not primarily relationships of size – experienced by the obser-ver at the same time. Designed to fit the context of the observer's whole experience, variations in scale are a special and powerful expressive instrument. With good judgment, they may be intro-duced without evoking the sterilizing clinical speculations about sheer size.

Large and small scale may be described as simple situations of confrontation – I am standing before a building, it is larger than I expected it to be . . . etc. This is the convenient method that we have been using in order to indicate the variations typified by the apparent largeness or smallness of a human figure as it is seen against the architectural background: colossal scale, very large, large, normal, small, very small, toy scale. In these confrontations, the observer's first impressions of size and his expectations of size are conditioned by previous impressions of size. These, in turn, have been conditioned by impressions prior to them. Largeness or smallness of scale is always relative to a spectator's continuing experiences of size. This was shown in the example of the visitor in Rome, who found that his large-scale apartment made him feel a little smaller than usual, and was a little impressive. For after a week or two he found himself accepting this standard of scale as normal for residential use. Variations in the continuity of impres-sions of size – both the degree of continuity and the way that it is achieved – are the warp upon which the woof of large-small scale are woven; and they are equally important to a scale treatment.

We have already considered the continuity of impressions of size as it affects basic perception. To organize any view as a portion of the real world, the spectator must form a conception of the way that the shapes relate to his own size, or to the size of some familiar object. To fully experience even a small building, literally thousands of views must be organized – not by a systematic wiping of the structure by the eyes, but by gathering cues from views scattered near and far, focused and wide. To do this efficiently, the conception of relative size formed in one view must be conveyed to the next, and to the next. This standard of size, of which the observer is scarcely aware, helps him to organize this complicated experience into an understandable whole. Where, at the one extreme, it is almost impossible to apply a continuing standard of size to that which is seen, perception may be so difficult as to discourage participation.

The recent fashion for box-like structures and simple surfaces led to the design of many buildings that inadequately control a spectator's impressions of size. Seen across the roof tops, or from down the street, these big boxes are at one moment seen at large scale – like models of themselves. The next moment, the full size is appreciated; but in another glance, the large-scale version is reinstated. The cause of these fluctuating impressions of size lies in the failure to introduce large subordinate shapes between the box-like over-all shape of the building and the fine-drawn demarcations of the glass walls. When attention is drawn to the fine linear divisions, their relationship to the whole shape is lost. When attention is focused upon the over-all box, the fine subdivisions are ineffective. In other, very similar, buildings the structural frame is clearly stated as a larger unit, or some other breakdown has been found, and this peculiar fluctuation of experience is avoided. The same effect may be observed in the Kresge Auditorium at M.I.T., where the instability of the scale treatment is complicated by the instability of a triangular shape that is very different seen from the flat, or seen from the point.

The fluctuation of size impressions, according to the spectator's viewpoint, or through accidents of illumination and foreground, is for some of us a familiar aspect of the environment. Most of our larger cities have blocks in which it is impossible to relate impressions of size in any very coherent way; and which, in effect, produce spot-shot visual experience with wildly unstable standards

107

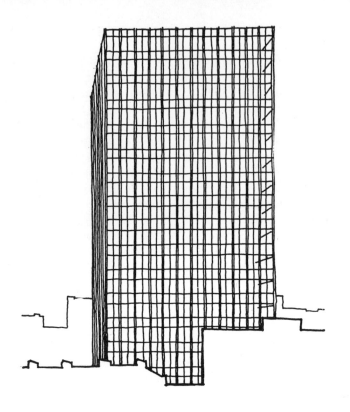

Seen across the roof tops . . .

of size. A city block of this kind may juxtapose old brownstone houses, in a slightly enlarged residential scale; parking lots that are in a large scale when they are empty and a smaller scale when they are full of cars; and loft buildings that firmly announce a large scale, on the street side – with considerable feeling of bigness – and on the other sides lapse into huge blank walls, alternately seen as small 'models of themselves', or as much larger. One needs only to throw into the collection one well designed modern building in rather small scale – combined with great feeling of bigness – sitting in a dream-like isolation of self-containment.

The effects of this lack of control within a building, or sprawling across the city, should be studied. The most obvious result is the fact that one must take in the environment in spite of the size

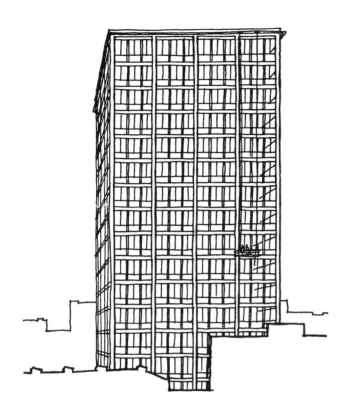

the structural frame is clearly stated

impressions that are conveyed. In the absence of some other incentive, the spectator cannot be expected to work at perception. In this case, he is likely to use his eyes to avoid traffic and to get where he is going, while his mind and emotions are turned inward. If he glances at what is before him, he may pick out – and see as fragments – those parts of the building or of the city block that interest him.

Now discouragement by confusing the eye and fragmentation of larger designs into smaller parts, may contribute to a design. Camouflage may be used to play down unsightly objects. Fragmentation may be used to reduce a large design to small scale, or to emphasize parts of it that should be distinguished. But when they occur accidentally, they prevent intensive participation. In the design of a city block, they prevent the block's being experi-

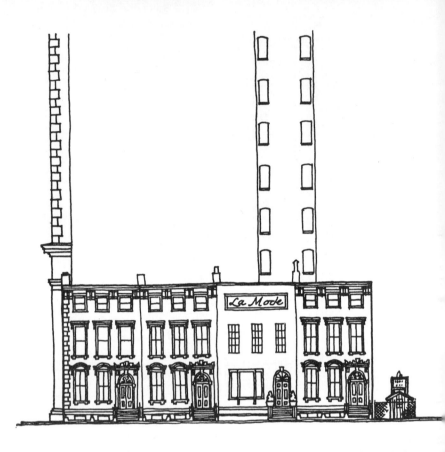

Most of our larger cities have blocks in which it is imposs

enced as a coherent whole, and discourage meaningful differentiation. At the same time, they allow very little correspondence
between the different scale treatments and the meanings a spectator may reasonably attach to what he sees.

The accidental views that indicate widely fluctuating scales are
the most harmful. They shock and surprise, inviting clinical
analysis. And they may degrade visual experience from 'reality',
accepted without question, to an arbitrary tricking of the eyes. It is
only when an observer may assume that his impressions of size
are what they appear to be that he is able freely to accept his
direct experience of a design, and to perceive it vividly and completely.

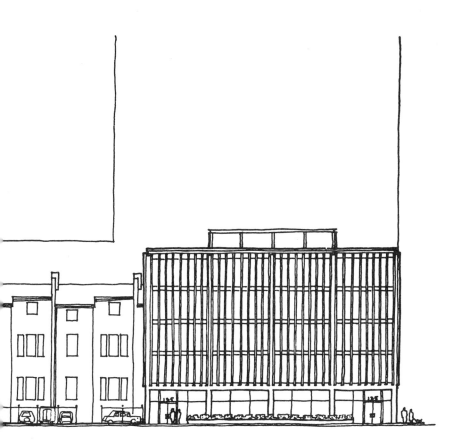

e impressions of size in any very coherent way

Let us contrast this fluctuating experience with a controlled city block that affords the minimum ease of perception which an observer needs to relax and take in his surroundings, to discover a continuity between size impressions, and to find a correspondence between impressions of size and meaning. This is accomplished when the impressions of size are controlled so as to be always what the observer expects. In the example of a 'fluctuating' single building, we have already seen that this could be accomplished by the accentuation of a large 'measuring' unit of the structural frame. With this intermediate size, the observer looking at the fine drawn mullion divisions cannot fail to relate them to the bolder demarcations of the bay system. And when he

111

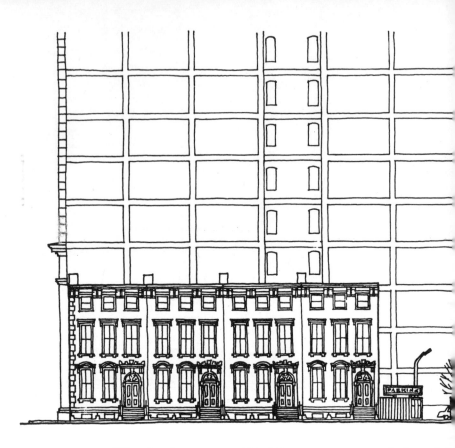

What has been accomplished is a mere accommodation of th

looks at the whole box shape, these big intermediate units are clearly stated and the ladder of sizes is completed. In the design of a city block, we must expect the means to control impressions of size to be more complicated. Suppose the row of brownstone residences is unbroken, evoking one scale, and the parking lot is divided with planting and fences, or depressed, so that – full or empty – it pretty constantly suggests a single scale. The blank walls of the loft building may be controlled by brick patterns and a statement of the structural frame; and the new building may very well have a somewhat less precious scale and less feeling of bigness – why should an office building be so high-strung?

There do not have to be any fluctuating views in which the

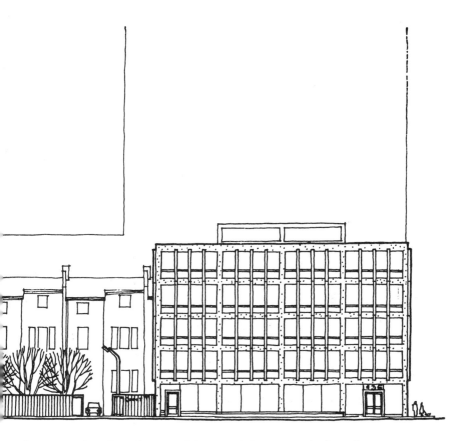

impression of size accidentally shifts; and the differences in scale can be 'as expected'. If the scale varies a little from building to building, this need not be surprising. If the warehouse is a little large in scale, it will seem appropriate to its largely inanimate function. If the houses are a little smaller scaled, this is because they have their real significance as house units. In short, although the design of the whole city block may not be very rewarding, the impressions of size in one view may be carried throughout, with only the variations that are expected, and probably unnoticed. Perception is easier, the spectator may relax and enjoy it; and the continuities of his experience are apt to coincide with the meaning attached to what is seen. If the loft building is difficult to organize

115

with the houses, does it not also serve very different functions? If the loose nature of the design holds little incentive to see the block as a whole, it nevertheless allows it to be seen for what it is: a juxtaposition of different structures in the same world. Even a shocking change of scale may be introduced 'as expected' without disrupting this continuity. A power plant might stand at the block's end, executed in a very large scale, and its visual detachment from the neighbourhood – due to the contrast in scale – might be a satisfactory expression of the fact that it serves the whole quarter of the town and not merely the block that it is in.

This rough control of scale is the minimum for a humane environment. The 'remodelled' city block is a place in which people may live without damage to their sensibilities and engage in a healthy give and take with the visible world. But it is something less than architectural design at its most effective. What has been accomplished is a mere accommodation of the observer's expectations, in order to achieve a minimum continuity of experience. The architect is by no means limited to following expectations. Through the design itself, he has at his disposal the means to create expectations as well as to follow them. The buildings that surround an observer are, after all, the present and the most recent conditioner of his expectations. Indeed, we have already seen that where architecture surrounds him, it partly determines his preconceptions concerning the normal appearance of people and recognizable sizes in the architectural setting. To a remarkable extent, what an observer expects, and the continuity of his experiences of size, can be controlled by the architect in design. This is fortunate. It is only tolerable to live in a world that can be comfortably seen, that you can easily take in, and that allows you to accept size impressions for what they seem to be. Fine architecture goes further. It creates an environment that the spectator may respond to, which actively engages his mind and emotions, and which invites him to feel about and to understand his surroundings. We shall consider the full implications of this difference later. But first, let us see how an architect may create, as well as reflect, the observer's preconceptions of size and continuity.

Carrying Power,
Sequence and Framing

Early in our discussion of human scale, we commented on the reciprocal effects of a building's system of bays and divisions.[30] In order to measure the building, the divisions are used to spread the recognizable sizes of the human figure, and other shapes, throughout the design, and to firmly incorporate the shapes that give equivocal impressions of size. The same divisions influence the observer's conception of a normal relationship between the recognizable sizes of people, familiar shapes, and the architecture – more divisions lead him to expect that they will be smaller against the architecture, fewer divisions cause him to expect them to be larger. Thus, the system of divisions that is designed to measure a building for an observer, in turn, influences his standard of measurement. But whether the divisions are size-distributing or size-suggesting, their influence is prescribed by the observer's eventual measurement of the building, through close personal experience and by a careful study of the design.

When a building is designed in human scale, as we first defined it,[31] there is a single standard of measure which remains unchanged no matter how long or how closely the building is studied. The divisions of the design have been made to carry the standard of the human figure to the whole building; and they have the effect of always suggesting to a spectator the same standard of human measure. Abnormally large scale or small scale, in the cases that we have so far examined, must be used in a 'cushioned area'. This is where the observer's expectations match the discrepancy between the two standards of measure: one suggested by the building's division system, and the other eventually established through familiarity and close study. In the example of a

[30] Pp. 84–87 above.
[31] See p. 70 above, 'A simple description of the idea of human scale . . .'

On the door step . . .

at a little distance

church, we found that the way that the people understand and feel about its functions leads them to expect a somewhat larger than usual scale. The expectation cushions and absorbs the discrepancy in standards of size, and it may even be heightened and dramatized through definitely large-scale or small-scale treatments. But this freedom to manipulate the scale of a building derives from expectations that the observer formed before his first experiences of the design. We must discover how the design itself can make discrepancies in size standards acceptable. And to do this, we must have a closer look at the way that a spectator perceives the scale-regulating shapes of a design.

To be effective, a division system must be seen and read. Buildings are usually seen at a variety of distances, rather than from fixed positions; and a viewer reads their scale treatment in the shapes and colours that are distinct at his distance from them. Consequently, for any scale treatment, the carrying power of the shapes that are used very much determines the effect. To be certain of the way that specific architectural elements will carry at various distances, it is necessary to study what will be before the eyes in each view. But some general remarks about the carrying power of shapes and colours are useful. As a rule, the shapes that may be seen and read from a great distance are large, simple, and project boldly, so that they create shade and cast deep shadows. The bigness and boldness is needed to create a definite figure that will carry through the blue of the atmosphere and will be clearly seen when small in the view. Small and complicated shapes do not carry as well. And where they are flat and cast no shadows, or cast broken shadows, they tend to be legible only when seen from close up. At a distance, the haze of the atmosphere blurs and smudges them and the eye must strain in order to catch the fine detail. Colours that contrast with the colours of the site, or which reflect much light, will usually carry further. Those that absorb light, or melt into the surrounding colours, may be easily distinguished only from near by.

The scale of a building is seldom controlled by a single set of shapes that is equally telling from a great distance, from middle distance, and from nearby. Even in a small room where there are no distant views, the designer must think of the scale as conveyed by different shapes at different distances. The unusually short views, at arm's length, assume a considerable importance when the observer is confined at close range with the colours and shapes around him. Similarly, the top of a tower will not ordinarily be seen at close range; but it will probably have to be designed for unusually long distances as well as for moderately long views. Where there are neither unusually long views nor exceptionally close ones, as in the design of an ordinary house, there remains a significant transfer of influence from one set of shapes to another, as the spectator approaches or moves away from the building. If the house is to be designed in strict human scale, so that a human figure will always appear normal against it, this uniform standard of measure must be suggested by a different rank of shapes at each viewing distance.

On the doorstep, the spectator's views may be dominated by the regular riff of the wood siding and the fragments of the door and window mouldings that fall within his view. At a little distance from the house, the boards will be seen as an over-all texture and the mouldings will be absorbed into the larger shapes of window and door rectangles. His view at this distance may be dominated by a window unit – the pattern of light mullions against the dark void, neatly contained in the frame. A little further from the building, his view may be most influenced by the regular pattern of openings in the whole wall, and by the broad sweep of the eaves line. Still further back, from across the street, these shapes may lose their interest, and the whole profile of the building, crowned by the roof and chimney shapes, may be most easily seen as a single shape against the landscape.

A consistent standard of size throughout this experience must be implemented by successive ranks of shapes that are most easily seen at different distances. Some grow powerful, while others fade from prominence as the observer moves toward, or draws away from, the building; and the control of scale is transferred from one set of dominant shapes to the next. The 'telescopic' arrangement of divisions that was recommended as a distribution system for sizes[32] takes into account this aspect of the spectator's experience. The organization of one set of divisions within another, which is in turn within another, may provide a set of predominant shapes for each viewing distance. And as a free observer moves about, the transfer of influence from one set to another may be smoothly accomplished.

The simplest examples of the positive control that an architect may exercise over the observer's expectations makes use of the sets of shapes that dominate his size impressions at different dis-

[32] Pp. 77-79 above.

Regular pattern of windows and the broad sweep of the eaves line . . .

It may be most easily seen as a single shape

tances. Where the designer can predict with reasonable accuracy the scope and distance of views, he may design successive sets of shapes to influence the observer's conception of normal size and to build smooth transitions between different standards of size. This has been done in the famous Taj Mahal.

At a great distance it is little more than a silhouette, a very fine and complete shape in itself. The big simple dome is visually sup-

The full silhouette is still of great importance

It will grow in size with each step forward

ported at its base by lesser domes. The fine outline shape is in very large scale, as there are at this distance few details that can be seen to measure it. However, the impression of size is not uncontrolled, and it could not be mistaken for a small building. The two small domes and the double curved shape of the big dome give some measure of the size. And the trees, minarets and flanking pavilions show that it is a large structure. From within the gate the full silhouette, that is now completely shown, is still of great importance; and one might say that the gate is set at this distance so that it may be clearly seen within the enclosure. But this outline is filled in and measured by its division into domes, main block and podium, and further divided by the octagonal corners and the large arched openings in the block. At this point, the spectator, who first saw the building from afar, will discover that it is somewhat larger than he had supposed; and as he progresses toward the building it will gradually grow in size with each step forward. To keep the long path from becoming monotonous – and to 'measure' its length – it is interrupted halfway by a raised tank. This mirror platform provides a view of the cross axis and

121

fresh, reflected and raised, views of the Taj before the axial approach is resumed. When the whole silhouette becomes uncomfortably large within the view, the flat face of the main block becomes more important, and the grand shapes of the central arched opening, flanked by smaller openings, dominate the view. The smaller alcoves measure the great central one, just as the smaller domes gave some appreciation of the size of the main dome. When the observer is so near that he cannot conveniently see the whole flat lower face, his attention will be dominated by the cavernous arches; and the details of the openings and panels within them begin to count substantially. These are so small in relation to the alcove, and so finely detailed, that they measure the arches as very big indeed; and the observer experiences an acceleration of the large-scale release of power. Where the axis approaches the platform there is another interruption. First the observer's view of the lower half of the building is cut off by the panelled wall of the podium, then he enters a stairway which encloses him until he climbs to the platform level. In the nearest views, from the platform, the big central alcove is too large in the view to be easily seen as an entirety. And at this distance the fine inlaid marble work and the sculptures in low relief begin to tell. They are not only framed by the big alcove but, in a sense, designed to fit within it rather than to fit the whole park before it. These patterns, and the fine details of the grilles and door mouldings, control the spectator's impressions as he enters the building.

Several things may be observed about this sequence, and about approach sequences in general. In this design the architect has arranged that the spectator's impressions, as he approaches the building, will have a planned sequence from very large scale to a greatly diminished large scale. It is not a regular progression, but is planned to jump in scale twice – once as you enter the gate, and again as you approach the building, very likely on the podium. This last jump occurs, specifically, when the fine detail within the alcoves becomes important in the view. Preparation for it is supplied by other fine details, for example those at the top and base of the dome and above the great central arch. Some of the true size of a large-scale building will eventually be discovered in any treatment. Here it is 'fed' to the spectator in a smooth progression, jumped at the end.

The sequence of views approaching the Taj Mahal varies from a very large-scale treatment to a smaller one, so that the viewer is shown the great size of the building in a controlled revelation.

This is, perhaps, the most common treatment for large buildings that are intended to impress. But it by no means exhausts the possibilities. The successful houses of Frank Lloyd Wright are apt to present the reverse sequence. At a distance they look quite large (for houses), and this impression is reinforced by great feeling of bigness. As you approach them, they diminish somewhat; and standing before the entrance door you find that the eaves and the door above you are quite low and very small in size, as measured by the bricks, boards, and your own eye height. I suspect that this small scale is often the consequence of a kind of greediness on the part of the designer: the desire to crowd many architectural elements into a small building. But as a plan of approach, the sequence can be gently disarming. The deflation of pretentions to size contributes to the unmistakably domestic character of the house, which 'softens up' as you walk toward it.

Another successful use of such a descending scale when approaching a building is furnished by a charming house on the Severn River near Annapolis. From the water, its classical portico suggests a very grand mansion. As you walk toward it and the full length of the house emerges from behind the trees it shrinks with each step. And when you stand on the porch, the window sash,

Its classical portico suggests a very grand mansion

A most ordinary set of measuring shapes

bricks, and other details of the near view show that the portico
is a scant two stories high and no wider than the single room
behind it. The deflation of pretention is beguiling here because,
as in the Wright house, it adds a cosy domestic quality; but more
importantly, because in the close views we find that everything
is in a very normal scale. The small-scale first impressions were
created entirely by the familiar formal design and the essentially
scale-less portico. The small-scale first impressions do not suddenly
give way before a behind-the-scenes glimpse of fraudulent
measure. They are displaced, step by step, by a most ordinary set
of measuring shapes in the expected relationship to each other:
'normal' scale.

In other buildings the sequence has used the element of surprise. The great pyramids of Egypt are frequently found in discussions of scale, because of the brutal simplicity of their scale treatment. As first seen, they have great feeling of bigness, owing to the immaculately simple geometrical shape; and they are seen in large scale. They have no treatment to control the impressions of size, but their great size guarantees that they will look big, while their simplicity guarantees that this size will not be fully appreciated. As you approach one of them, its size is further indicated by the stones (originally there was a polished stone casing) and by comparison with the human figures, camels, etc. nearby. And when one stands at its base, it is impossible not to be overawed by the pile's great size. But nothing has been done to help you grasp the full immensity; and its bigness has to be discovered – not once, but over and over again. The effect is somewhat crushing, but wholly in keeping with its function as a religious symbol, and as a tomb.

Something of the same experience, more smoothly regulated, is furnished by the approach to St. Peter's in Rome – another immense building. Here a colossal scale is controlled and maintained. It looks very big at first glance, and as you approach it, grows steadily in apparent size. But the smaller shapes that might have been used to revise the scale downward as you approach have been deliberately suppressed. The full size may be calculated by comparison with human figures, parked buses, etc., only to slip away again so that it must be repeatedly discovered. A perfunctory 'feeler' of elements in a reduced scale is supplied at the door (like a vestige of the scale reduction in the near view of the Taj Mahal) by the metal gates. But walking through the door is still rather like passing between the legs of parked elephants. In this case, as in the case of the great pyramid, the surprising size finds a proper object in the building's meaning. Built as the centre of Christendom, it was intended to overawe. Designed in the grand operatic style, the bravura of surprising sizes is in harmony with the great outstretched arms and the majestic sweep of the shapes.

Obviously, the architect may plan sequences of scale that control rooms or courtyards as well as views approaching a building. It is elegantly done in some seventeenth century town houses. The large scale of the street front precedes the forecourt, which is only slightly reduced in scale. From this, you enter an entrance hall that maintains a large scale – reduced, but near that of the courtyard. In this way, the transition from the street into the building is a progression from public to private scale, but gradually accomplished so as to be continuously experienced. The big drawing rooms will be in a smaller, definitely interior, scale. Now that you have been 'received', the scale will be more gracious. And if you penetrate into the boudoir, you will discover the flattering small scale that encourages intimacy. All of this is done with considerable finesse as becomes people who were, after all, accustomed to evaluating every nuance and to grading their good morning bows to the rank of the person before them.

What is of interest in all of these sequences is the fact that the architect may use the set of shapes that dominates the observer's view at a particular distance to bend or to alter the standard of size 'expected'. He may use the different emerging sets of shapes to support a uniform standard of size; or he may plan a varied sequence in which one scale treatment, seen from afar, is smoothly developed into another scale treatment, seen close up. He may place light breaks in scale where they fit the over-all meaning of the design – its formal arrangement, and preconceptions about it. And in those rare instances where surprise and wonder about size contribute to the meaning of the design, he may even use the sequence of views to prepare and to spring surprising jumps in scale – from one scale treatment to another, or from an exaggerated scale to an eventual re-evaluation.

There are limits to the general rules that can be drawn from these sequences. The spectator's experience in each design depends on the total effect of the architecture and its surroundings, as well as on the treatment of sizes. However, if the reader will make allowances for the arbitrary factor in observations that are made out of context, a number of interesting general comments may be made. First, in approaching a building it is clear that successive sets of shapes that progress from one kind of scale to another involve much more than the large-scale or small-scale experience that is offered at the different distances. There is also present a dynamism of controlled change in scale which is, in itself, very powerful and persuasive. Where it is a smoothly controlled 'curved' transition from one treatment of scale to another, the shifting of the normal relationship between building and observer has a drama that can only be compared to the retarding and accelerating of the time measure in music. Like the rubato of music, the success of the effect depends very much on the smoothness with which it is done.

This analogy may be extended to a second comment about scale variations in the approach to a building. Where the architect fails to control the evolution from one scale to the other, and the spectator alternately organizes what is before his eyes as first in one scale and then as in another, the fluctuating experience is very similar to arbitrary and senseless tempo changes in music. In both music and architecture, the effect upon the spectator is to discourage his acceptance of what his senses present to him as 'real', and to call clinical attention to the mechanics of the performance. We saw this illustrated in the case of the tin-can skyscraper and the typical chaotic city blocks.[33] In both examples, the spectator found that his interpretation of the shapes before his eyes arbitrarily shifted from one standard to another and then back again. The skyscraper resembled a model of itself, then was seen at a smaller scale, then looked bigger, and again offered the large-scale interpretation. Under the circumstances it is not possible to anticipate the kind of sequence. What is seen at one distance cannot be used to prepare the spectator for a somewhat different scale that may be suggested by the set of shapes dominating the view at another distance. The sudden jump, with neither transitional development nor meaning that the observer can associate with the sudden change of scale, is perceptual nonsense.

A third comment on the dynamic approach sequences – in which one treatment of scale evolves into another – needs particularly to be regarded as a rule that has many exceptions in the context of a design. This is the influence, upon the treatment of scale, of designing for carrying power, or legibility, at a distance. The large shapes, with the bold projections and deep shadows that are needed to make a building read from a great distance, make it easier to design the distant views in a scale larger than that of the closer views. Similarly, the small broken flat shapes that read clearly from nearby lend themselves to small-scale treatment; the small shapes supply the bottom rungs that complete the ladder of size distribution. Consequently, where a building is only seen from a narrow street, or where the spectator is confined in a small room, the smaller shallower formal arrangements – that are comfortably seen from close up – tend to make it easier to design in a small scale. Where there is no other object in mind, one commonly discovers that on approaching a building the scale alteration curve begins with a large scale, becomes smaller

[33] Pp. 107–110 above.

*Must often be skilfully designed against the tendency of the shapes
to become illegible from afar*

in scale (i.e. the building looks larger as one approaches it), and
quite often diminishes rapidly at the doorway, where a spectator
goes up to the building and enters. The sequence is suitable to
buildings that are intended to impress, but not to annihilate.

It would be ridiculous to assume that, because they are common
and conveniently accommodate the design of shapes to carry at
various distances, variations on this curve would be desirable in
any particular design. The conformation should be recognized
because it stakes out three problems of scale that cannot be readily
solved unless they are clearly seen. The maintenance of a uniform
scale in a sequence of views – as in our example of an ordinary
house – requires the design to maintain a single scale treatment,
at a distance and close up, against the tendency of the formal
arrangement to shift scales slightly. The effect of small scale at a

*Must be skilfully maintained against the tendency of the formal
arrangement to lose the observer's interest*

considerable distance must often be skilfully designed against the
tendency of the shapes to become illegible from afar. The effect of
large scale seen close up must usually be skilfully maintained
against the tendency of the formal arrangement to lose the observer's interest and attention.

Because different sets of shapes control the spectator's impressions
of size at different distances, the scale of the architecture surrounding a room or an open square does not directly determine the scale
of the space enclosed. Of course, the buildings along the side of a
city square *do* influence the observer's idea of its size and character. When they are in large scale, the space tends to appear somewhat smaller than it is, and to acquire the effects that are typical

of large-scale designs. The reduced size, grandeur, and latent power of St. Peter's square in Rome, for example, are qualities that the open space largely acquires from the surrounding buildings. Where the buildings are in small scale, the full size of an open square tends to be appreciated, and it tends to acquire qualities that are attributes of small scale. The extraordinary intimacy, combined with feeling of bigness, that is developed in the arcades of the Alhambra's Lion Court, is lent to the courtyard space. Nevertheless, the scale of the surrounding buildings is not identical with the scale of the open space that they define; and in some designs it substantially departs from it. The open space determines the viewing distances that a spectator is allowed. The carrying power of the architectural shapes determines the set of elements that will be legible at one distance or another. And the size that the spectator attributes to the open space, as opposed to the masses surrounding it, depends on his impressions at different distances. The trio of factors – viewing distances, surrounding architecture, and the space enclosed – may be related so as to produce widely different impressions of scale.

At the extremes we may notice that the scale of the surrounding buildings may not fit the space defined. Where a small courtyard is enclosed by shapes that are in large scale, with the bold projections and large sizes that carry well at a distance, the spectator is subjected to impressions that are inescapably conflicting. He is made conscious of the longer distances and greater dimensions that the enclosing walls suggest, and at the same time he cannot escape the smallness of the enclosure. In fact, the enclosed space may exclude most of the distance for which the walls appear to be designed. The sensation evoked by this impression may still be felt for blocks, while walking through the old canyon streets of lower New York. A part of the discomfort derives from the suggested 'push' of the walls; but it also derives from the discrepancy between the measure of size, suggested by the enclosure, and the small area enclosed. To see the walls properly, the observer would have to step back into space that is outside the courtyard. Like most unpleasant sensations, this treatment may be used effectively in designs that expressively employ the tensions that are set up. But the effect carries with it a suggestion that the defining shapes do not fit the space enclosed; and its successful use appears to be limited to those designs in which an uneasy feeling of maladjustment is appropriate.

At the other extreme, a very large open square may be sur-

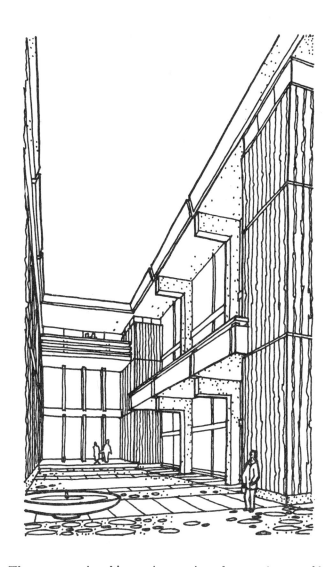

The spectator is subject to impressions that are inescapably
conflicting

rounded by buildings that do not 'fit' it, because they are quite
small in scale, and the shapes are illegible at a distance. Walking
around the perimeter of the square, the spectator may find that
the nearby buildings are pleasantly and intimately related to him-
elf; but he will find it difficult to relate the buildings seen from

*Buildings that do not 'fit' it because they are small in scale and the
shapes are illegible at a distance*

close up to those that he sees across the square. And when he walks
into the centre of the square, he will discover that his size impressions are inadequately controlled. The surrounding blocks of
buildings, their details blurred by distance and small in the view,
may read much smaller than they are. This will be particularly
apt to happen when rain or mist make the atmosphere thick. But
when the sun strikes one of the blocks, or when the point of view
is favourable, the size may again be fully appreciated and the
buildings and square may again appear enlarged.

Throughout a square of this kind, the spectator finds the buildings only casually related to the space that they enclose. When he
walks around the perimeter, the scale may be thought of as just
adequately determined; but when he ventures out into the centre
area, it is clear that the small-scale buildings do not adequately
control his impressions of size. This treatment may be satisfactory
when the designer wishes smaller building units to be appreciated
separately, rather than as an ensemble. A village green, or a
shopping centre, might be designed in this fashion in order that

The statues and elevated urns are invaluable

each house or each store may command the spectator's full attention in the near views, without competition. But in these instances it might be wise to kill the central area by filling it, or dividing it, with trees.

Because the scale of an open space is not identical with the scale of the buildings that define it, the ground plane is of the greatest importance in the scale treatment of large open spaces; and in the design of large rooms, the ceiling may be extremely important. The contribution to scale of the fussy parterre plantings of Baroque gardens – which are, as a rule, difficult to defend as patterns or as vegetation – may be appreciated when one compares the gardens in which they remain, to those from which they have been removed. They carry a fine small measuring unit out into the open space, where the smaller divisions of the buildings are less telling. But the elements that are most effective in the middle of large open spaces are those that rise above the ground to confront the viewer. At Versailles, the statues and the elevated urns are invaluable in controlling impressions of size from the open terraces around the chateau. And they are particularly important adjuncts to the building, which lacks carrying power commensurate with its final extended size. In St. Mark's Square in Venice the same control is extended, as a sort of scale governor, by the paving patterns and the elaborate lamp standards. In the large city square that we have been examining – surrounded by small-scale buildings with little carrying power – the treatment of the ground plane and the objects that rise in the central space may be decisive. Where the small scale of the buildings is carried throughout the square by the landscaping and paving, the building blocks will be properly evaluated when seen from a distance. Where the planting and paving support a larger scale, appropriate to the big volume enclosed, the surrounding buildings may appear to be subordinate units of a larger whole.

We have seen that the scale of a group of buildings may fail to 'fit' the scale of the space that they surround, because of the scale of the architectural shapes, or because of their carrying power. By a fine adjustment of these same factors, they may be made to fit exactly; and this may be accomplished in a variety of ways. First of all, the carrying power of the shapes may be adjusted to fit the viewing distances that are available. For a small court the shapes and colours may be relatively flat, small, or broken up, in order to be read from near by and from the moderate distances within the walls. For a large square these same arrangements may be used for the near views, but additional sets of shapes will be needed for legibility from moderate distances and from the extreme long views across the square. The scale in either instance may be large, normal, or small. Because of the relationship that we have discussed between largeness of scale and carrying power, it will be easier to design the small court in a relatively small scale; and it will be convenient to design the large square in a definitely large scale. But with care, the designer is free to develop the scale that seems appropriate to him. When he chooses to maintain the same scale throughout the space, it will be accomplished by different sets of shapes seen at different distances; and in the case of the large open space, it will probably be accomplished through the development of the ground plane and shapes introduced out in the space.

But the architect is also free to plan variations in the scale that are similar to the variations that we found in views approaching a building. In a small space, the variations will have to be slight, corresponding to the limited choice of viewing distances. In the Lion Court of the Alhambra, for example, a small jump in scale between the near views and the longest ones available supports the unusual feeling of bigness in this delicately adjusted small-scale design. Within the arcades, the fine plaster work and slender columns develop a maximum of intimacy and personal relationship. A tile wainscot originally added to this effect. But as you look across the court from between the columns, or as you stand out in it, the scale is not quite so small. The simple roofs, the simple surfaces of the pavilions that rise above the cloister, and the gravel court floor with its crossed water channels and central fountain, suggest a slightly larger scale for the whole court. The transfer from one norm of scale to the other is made smooth by the predominance of near objects framing distant ones (columns and fountain) and, above all, by the rapid washing out of the fine plaster reliefs with distance, which turns them into relatively simple textured flat surfaces.

A larger version of this scheme – an intimate scale close-up, becoming a larger scale as seen from across the space – is supplied by a post-war shopping square in Munich, Germany. Here, the painted decorations on the old tower, and the elaborate hanging signs contained under a strong canopy, quickly disappear at a distance, leaving a bolder large scale design.

With care, the architect may also make the one side of a square in one scale and another in a different scale. This is done in thousands of public squares, where there are large and important buildings facing more ordinary ones. Perhaps the most polished example is the little square of San Ignazio in Rome, where this scale treatment – and also the shape of the enclosure – has been used to make the 'far carrying' shapes of the church front at home in a very small square. Other open spaces, St. Mark's Square in Venice, or the Close at Salisbury, are extremely complicated in their scale treatment. They not only use different scales at different sides but use the carrying power and scale of the buildings to state their proper meaning, as institutions, in a complex of related institutions. But before we are prepared to examine them we must examine the designer's other means for predetermining the observer's expectations.

The shift from bottom to top is treated as a transition from plain to complex

The architect may mould an observer's expectations right before his eyes. Time, and a few steps, separate the changes of scale from far to near distances, and from room to room. But the same control may be accomplished in no more time than it takes an observer to organize his views, standing still. Consider the excellent example of a fine medieval tower design. It is quite large in scale at the base, which is broken only by the large buttress shapes, a strong base course and the stone joints; and it is much smaller in scale at the top, which is crowned by a spire of stone lacework. The shift between bottom and top is treated as a transition from plain to complex, and from large scale to a smaller scale at the top. This has the effect of heightening the tower, because the smaller-scale top looks higher than it is. And it acquires a dynamic rocket-like upward movement – and great feeling of bigness – from the smoothly evolving change of scale and complexity. The top will often be seen only at a distance, of course, and as a rule the base will only be seen from close up. But even when one can stand off and embrace in one wide view both top and bottom (taking in both large-scale and small-scale parts of the design), there is no surprising break in the experience; and the effects of large and small scale, respectively, persist. The reason lies in the care with which the transition between the two has been designed. It is impossible to experience the different scales without also experiencing the visual reason for the difference – a smooth transition, without breaks, that is essential to the formal scheme of the design.

By arrangements of this kind, the formal design may lead people to expect a scale variation in very much the way that we have found different functions, or different techniques of construction, lead them to expect various standards of size. The observer is being led from one standard of scale to another by the smooth transition of scales between them; and it is done before his eyes without damaging surprises. In mature Gothic architecture, this variation is usually applied to the main body of the church outside, and to the interior as well as to the towers. In the up and down direction, these changes are in a favoured position of being measured by people, small houses, carts, etc., only at the large-scale end of the stick. However, the same modulation in scale is often used from side to side, with a little more discretion. Notice the modulation between main Chateau and its dependencies at Vaux-le-Vicomte. It is not very smoothly done, but the variation in scale is backed up by an obvious and significant distinction as to function. A similar differentiation through treatment of scale may be seen in the Unesco Building in Paris, where the larger scale of the meeting rooms, in keeping with their significance, is used to counteract the bulk of the office block.

A more complex game of central pile and smaller scale dependencies is played splendidly at Blenheim Palace. Here, as at Vaux-le-Vicomte, you will notice that there is a larger scale for the central block (not a very large scale, but with great feeling of

A smaller-scale colonnade is brought up in a semi-circular sweep

bigness) and there are smaller-scale wings. But you will see that a smaller-scale colonnade is brought up in a semi-circular sweep to accentuate the size and scale of the squared central portico; and smaller-scale wings are interrupted by pavilions, whose larger scale links them to the main pile. Thus, the fragmentation of the design by changes in scale is used to create an order easily understood and grasped – punctuating the vast group of buildings. Because it is easily understood as a central block with dependencies, and as a 'sonata' arrangement of different scales, the drama of formal emphasis and change of scale may actually be used to clarify and simplify what might have been a monotonous barracks – too complex and large to be easily assimilated. Inability to differentiate in this manner, because of repeated additions, makes Versailles a dull building, saved only by the brilliant garden design.

The use made of sequences at Blenheim takes us a little ahead of our explorations. The design employs a device for variation in scale that I shall call scale framing, as opposed to sequential variations in scale. It is the setting of one scale within the context of another, and framing the necessary transition. The way that it may be done is perhaps best shown in a detail. In fact, it is mentioned only in 'Beaux Arts' writings in connection with ornamen-

*The jump in scale
still exists*

tation, although it has a much more important application.[34]

Suppose that I wish to introduce into the design of a big room a fine piece of sculpture, or a handsome marble panel. This will usually be in a scale smaller than the scale of the room design, because a sculpture is likely to be broken up into fine gradations of shade and projection, and marble is apt to be reduced by the colour areas and intricate veining patterns. The problem is how to introduce these elements while maintaining the larger scale of the room as a whole, so that there is no uncontrolled experience of surprise. The solution may be to set the sculpture in a niche that is in the larger scale of the whole room, or to set off the marble by a border or moulding that is a big rectangle in scale with the whole room. When this is done, the jump in scale still exists, but it is framed by a large-scale shape that encircles the gap, making it a hiatus that, in its effect on the design, is not very different from a window or door opening. A change of material or surface treatment helps to make the change in scale 'expected'. Without

[34] John V. Van Pelt, *The Essentials of Composition as Applied to Art*, New York, 1913; Georges Gromort, op. cit.

doubt, one could make a greater change of scale with a bronze sculpture on a stone wall than with a stone one; or in a liver-coloured marble panel on a stone wall than a stone-gray panel. By the same token, the sculpture could embrace a greater jump than a flat panel, etc. There are endless variations in the device. The frame may be a transition, easing a smaller scale into the large scale surroundings. This is accomplished by big soft mouldings in the marble Louis XIV rooms at Versailles, for example, and in countless Gothic niches, where the niche opening is a self-transition in the scale, entirely relieving the statute of the burden. Changes of meaning may be used to ease the transition; and so may colour changes, material changes, wall to sculpture changes, etc. A full exploitation of this device – not only used to integrate a small-scale detail into a larger scale building, but also employed as a device with its own value of scale dynamism -- may be observed in many Baroque buildings and in late medieval architecture. A mature example is supplied in the charming pilgrimage church at Wies, Germany.

First of all we may observe that with the exception of the four cardinal focal points – two side altars, a choir gallery and the chancel arch – the whole interior is in a larger scale at the bottom, and diminishes as it ascends, so that the top is dominated by the smaller scale of the ceiling painting. This is accomplished by the plainness of the column shafts and the exterior walls, and by the greater elaboration of the stucco arches and the architectural frame for the dome at the cornice level. Even the statues, at the base of each pair of columns, are handled with such a broad modelling that they resemble little wooden models blown up to a larger size. The colour scheme is graduated from the white of the walls and column shafts to the broken colour of the painted dome. Counter to this scheme of larger scale at the bottom and smaller and smaller as you ascend is the treatment of the four focal areas. The side altars, for example, are deliberately reduced in scale; and the change is handled primarily by 'framing'. The smaller-scale area of the altarpiece is surrounded by windows that set off its wall space, and then framed by its own vigorous silhouette and by its polychromy against the white wall. The entire smaller-scale area is fixed in the context of the whole room by a simple axial relationship. It is clearly something different, by position, by function, by shape and by colour; and it is not surprising to see that it is in a smaller scale.

Within the rather inexpertly designed altarpieces there is a

140

. . . Somewhat as though you were looking into a peep-show

continuation of the framing process. The altar table and the flanking columns are at a slightly larger scale than the ornaments within them; and they enclose a painting that is even smaller in scale. Because of this, the illusion of changing scales may be experienced somewhat as though you were looking into a peep show

– the smallest scale framed by a larger one, which is framed in the scale of the room. But it is firmly controlled as a planned hiatus in the larger continuity of scale. The arrangement may be compared to the late Gothic window that was introduced into the early medieval transept of Notre Dame at Paris. The wonderful glass and stonework is an obvious rift in the web of sizes, sapping the vigour of the entire transept end. Like the altarpieces at Wies, the new area is a hole in the ensemble of the interior. But this hiatus is without the buffer zone of transitional scale that would have softened the contrast; and it lacks the internal scale variations that would have reduced its formidable flatness. The final effect is not as disturbing as the photographs would indicate. There are colour variations that consolidate parts of the stone spider-web and introduce a pattern of larger areas. And the difference between a window and a wall, and the formal axial placing, lead one to tolerate the contrast.

At Wies, the scale variations are an inseparable part of the formal design, as they were at Blenheim Palace. They are in full agreement with the spatial conception of the interior. Indeed, it may be said that the framing of scale within scale, at the cardinal points and at the ceiling, is used to accentuate the scheme of spatial enclosure, release, and movement, around which the interior is designed. The altarpieces, through the nesting of scale within scale, supply a dynamic progression that substitutes for spatial escape. And the escape represented by the ceiling painting is given an extra lift and force by its framing in successive scales of plaster ornament. A similar deliberate use of variations in scale will be apparent when we return to the Taj Mahal, which we examined before as an approach sequence. There is a planned contrast in scale between the shapes within the arched alcoves and those outside them. This is the mechanism on which the jump in scale at the end of the approach sequence is based. It also provides, in a notably stable and serene building block, dynamic interest that could not be supplied solely by the recession of the alcoves. A gate to the Fort at Delhi provides a beautifully adjusted example of the same device. A modest entrance opening has been placed within a grand gateway; and the reduced scale of the area between entrance and gate arches, containing a small-scale window with a balcony, lends a dynamic movement to what is actually only a few feet of recession.

In less geometrical designs, the same skilful use of framing may be easily observed. Yet it is often extremely difficult to analyse

Some framing is absolutely necessary

exactly how it is done. In some Japanese garden designs, the shifting scales of foliage and stones are used to create dynamic interest and to suggest spatial escapes; but the treatment is freely devised, as sets of 'pictures' arranged along the spectator's path. It is particularly noticeable, to the extent that Japanese gardens are miniature symbolic landscapes, that some framing is absolutely necessary, whether the framing is done with the trees in the background, or with walls, or with raked sand borders. When one examines them (or the little mounds of Noguchi in the Prudential Insurance Company's courts), and compares them with some other fashionable uses of 'earth forms', it is apparent that framing makes the difference between a poetic evocation of landscape, on the one hand, and earth pimples on the other. Where earth shapes are in scale with the natural earth contours around them, that is of course another story.

The Prometheus court of Radio City provides a larger and bolder example of framing. The skating rink is usually filled with small-scale activity – skaters in the winter, and awnings, diners and greenery in the summer. The rectangular depression contains and frames a smaller scale within the larger-scale surroundings. Sometimes, when the sunken court is surrounded by flags or by plants, it acquires a transitional frame that eases the smaller scale activity into the larger scale surroundings. Of course, the largest examples of scale framing are found in urban plans, where skill in framing scales often determines whether a small landscaped area shall be lost, or shall exist happily, in a densely built-up area. Where it is abruptly surrounded by huge building blocks that are large or uncontrolled in scale, an intimate park or garden character seems unpleasantly and ineffectually fussy. But where the landscape is 'eased' into the architectural surroundings by a frame of smaller-scale structures or larger-scale trees, even a miniature landscape or a small garden may be made at home.

We began our discussion of human scale with the observation that impressions of size are illusion: they derive their final qualities from the relationships of sizes that are seen at the same time. And we based our first description of human scale upon the fact that the human figure, and other shapes which have recognizable sizes, eventually measure the architecture that is seen with them. For if a spectator is to be able to accept his visual impressions as 'reality', it must be possible to introduce these measuring rods into the architecture at any time without his being surprised at their apparent size. But the spectator's idea of the normal appearance of people and familiar shapes – seen against a building – fluctuates with his intellectual and emotional bias concerning the building's function, its place in the community, and even with its materials and method of construction. Where large-scale or small-scale designs coincide with his expectations, he may experience variations in scale – and eloquent expressive qualities – without a disastrous break into clinical speculation about sizes. Furthermore, the formal arrangement itself, as the present and most recent conditioner of the spectator's expectations, may be used to prepare him for different scales and for the dynamism of change in scale. Indeed, where the architect skilfully controls the environment, scale becomes a free design instrument for producing, as well as for reflecting, qualities of meaning and feeling.

Physical, Proportional, and Human Scales

Most of us take considerable pride in our own species, and we may even feel a warm glow of pleasure when we consider that the human figure is a unique standard of measure in architecture. But to understand architectural scale it is important to go beyond this flattering generality and to concentrate upon the reason why the human figure is of such value. It is because whatever the first impressions of a spectator, the human figure will ultimately measure the environment for him. It will eventually indicate a standard of size that is, or is not, continuously joined in the spectator's mind with previous size impressions. The continuity of this experience, and the observer's exploration of architecture as a part of the 'real' unquestioned environment, is the essential criterion of human scale. And in meeting this standard, the architect's treatment of the scale of buildings is not limited to the inflexible measure of a six-foot man. It is circumscribed only by the mind and emotions as found in complicated living people.

Strict human scale, as we first described it,[35] is contained within the broader definition of human scale that we have developed. That is to say, the architect who is able to think of normal scale as variable, and who can vary the scale of buildings according to the spectator's expectations, may easily design for the fixed standard of the human figure when he wishes to. And we may reasonably suppose that many buildings will require just this scale treatment. There is a similar relationship between our fully developed definition of human scale and the other conceptions of scale – as derived from physical requirements, or as a by-product of proportional systems – which we discussed earlier. Human scale may be considered a comprehensive conception that embraces what is valuable in these other approaches to scale; and this is one of the

---

[35] See p. 70 above.

traits that highly recommends it. Turning our attention again to physical scale and proportional systems, we will discover that they may play constructive parts in designing for human scale and may be considered contributing, rather than rival, points of view.

When a building's materials, structural system and disposition of useful space have been co-ordinated in an economical synthesis, they tend to provide the raw materials for human scale. The necessary divisions – from small units such as bricks, tiles or boards, to large ones such as structural bays and floor levels – provide a ladder of sizes from large to small. They are related by function, each accomplishing a necessary task in the most efficient way; and although the eye does not always find them systematically related, it tends to be able to. In an entirely functional warehouse design, for instance, the whole building is marked off into floors and bays by the light bands of the exposed concrete structural frame. Within each of the rectangular compartments there are two major divisions. The lower portion is filled with bricks – small units with a recognizable size – and capped by a sill, which has somewhat less definite implications of size. Over the brick panel, the space within the structural frame is filled with a window that is broken by mullions into smaller glass divisions and has a ventilating sash. The width of the mullions and the size of the concrete columns and girders of the frame reflect the nature of the materials used and the structural task performed by each member. Thus, there is a ladder of sizes from large to small, and a rational juxtaposition of shapes – some with definite recognizable sizes, others with tentative connotations of size. This order of shapes tends to supply the divisions that in human scale are needed to spread the influence of recognizable sizes to the whole building. And because it is a ladder of divisions, arranged the one within the other, it tends to afford sets of shapes that will control the spectator's impressions of size from different distances.

The exterior of a typical Gothic hall affords a similar practical synthesis that is as easily read by the eye. The length of the building is broken into bays by buttresses. The width of the buttresses, their projection from the wall, and their diminution as they rise, are roughly indicative of their size. Within the bays, the upper walls are filled with windows that are divided vertically by stone mullions, and horizontally by the less prominent iron bars to which the glass is wired. The number of mullions, their thickness, and their relationship to the bars, again is not a definite indication of a size; but it roughly suggests one. The wall below is measured

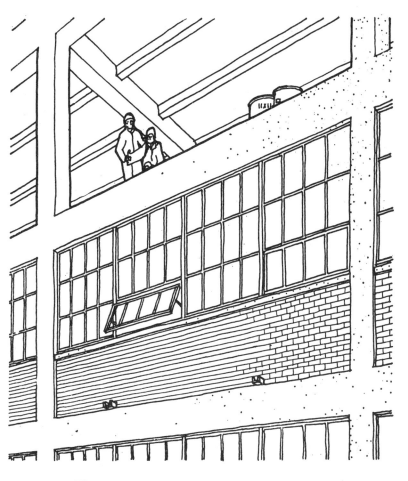

There is a ladder of sizes from large to small

by the large stones and the stone joints; and it has a moulded base where the wall thickens out toward its footing width. Here, as in the warehouse, the ladder of divisions from large to small provides the distribution system and furnishes the sets of shapes that are clearly read at different distances, which are needed for human scale. Often the designer will only have to appreciate, and to efficiently use, the peculiarities of his materials and of his mode of construction in order to establish a precise control of the building's scale.

Naturally, where the functional arrangement does not provide an adequate control of scale, he will have to adjust and alter it; and he may add some divisions and suppress others. In some cases, he will discover that the most practical arrangement of materials, structure, and useful space does not yield a ladder of sizes at all. It may be practical, for example, to wrap a fireproof wall around the whole interior arrangement and structural system. Or weather protection may make it desirable to cover up most of the essential elements. In these instances, the facing materials or the fabrication details of a screen wall may be exploited for scale. But the designer may also need to introduce larger, more important, shapes in order to control the spectator's size impressions. These missing shapes may often be found by representing the hidden divisions of the design. An indentation in a brick wall may represent the column hidden inside and, at the same time, provide a much needed rung in the ladder of sizes. A projecting belt course of brick may represent a covered girder and, at the same time, show the floor division.

The practical order of divisions is especially useful in the treatment of scale, because it tends to run throughout a building, spreading with it a measure of size. Structural columns, beams and girders may be shown, or represented, on all of the sides of the building, and their grid may penetrate into all of the rooms of the interior. The smaller measure of bricks, concrete textures, or wall panels, may appear and reappear wherever the observer happens to venture and to look.

A special value accrues to the scale treatment when it is based upon, and developed from, these practical divisions. Its visual statement gains additional authority from adhering to a practical necessity. Mere speculation about size impressions – as experiences that might have been arranged one way or another – is made improbable because the divisions that control the observer's impressions run throughout the building and they seem to be inevitable consequences of the practical arrangement. A rapid survey of architectural works will show that this fact has not always been appreciated. In fact, a scholarly case may be made for its invention not so long ago by Viollet-le-Duc. But a closer look tends to indicate, rather, that architects have shown their appreciation of the fact in complicated ways. Thus, the essential construction and the typical use of materials in the great medieval cathedrals largely derives from the visual design of the interiors; but every detail of these great luminous shells shows a fine appreciation of the coincidence between visual and practical divisions. Baroque archi-

Other scale-giving divisions must be designed to prevail

tecture, which often used downright playful walls – loaded with play columns and mock entablatures – and which usually dissolved into plaster phantasy in the interior, exhibits a persistent preference for visual divisions that coincide with the make-believe structural elements. In our own time, there is no major architect who does not seek this extra authority for visual design, and this extra economy of the design synthesis.

It is when the practical divisions of a design may be mistaken for what they are *not*, that they present scale problems. Under some circumstances, a hollow tile block may be mistaken for the much smaller brick; or a large window – with very big panes of glass and unusually thick mullions – may be mistaken at first glance for a smaller window. The handsome Refectory and Dormitory building at the Rhode Island School of Design shows that mistakes of this kind may appear even in a well designed building. In a distant view, the large ventilating stacks may suggest the familiar, and smaller, shape of ordinary chimneys. The simple stick-like shapes of the beams and columns, because they suggest the timbers of houses framed in much the same way, may momentarily appear much smaller than they are. In all of these instances, the other scale-giving divisions of the building must be designed to prevail against misunderstanding.

We may conclude that the physical order of materials, construction and useful space, are natural raw material for a building's scale treatment. And we may observe that these natural materials need to be designed twice – once as a practical way of building, and again as a system of dimensions controlling scale. If the two kinds of designing can be simultaneously executed, so much the better.

The proportional systems that we have surveyed may also be considered, in a sense, sub-species of human scale. They are not by origin; for we have seen that they are the ancestors, rather than the descendants, of human scale.[36] But the valuable qualities that the use of proportional systems may contribute to architectural scale may be secured while designing in human scale. To begin with the simplest kind of regulating system, we may observe that the Japanese modular system of beams, columns and mats, supplies a distributing system of sizes, within and outside a building, that is ready-made for human scale. And because the modules are uniform across most of Japan, they supply a design for human scale with a distribution system made up of recognizable sizes. The module used in Mies' Illinois Institute of Technology Campus, has a similar value for design in human scale. It does not have the advantage of national uniformity, as the Japanese module does; but it is used in an even more comprehensive fashion – extending to the spaces between buildings as well as to the interiors and exteriors.

The dimensions established by harmonic proportion systems appear to be about as useful to a human scale treatment as they are to contemporary architecture in general. The limitations, in either instance, lies in the spectators' being able to see and understand the ratios that are used. In a Palladian house the order – the system of columns, entablatures, etc. – is certainly seen; and it runs through the design as a useful size-distributing module. Where they can be recognized, the harmonic intervals governing the solid walls, window and door openings, and the whole shape of building blocks, furnish a regularity that helps the spectator to relate shapes with recognizable size to the larger shapes of the designs. And because these divisions are factors of the whole width or height of the building, they help him to relate the size of the parts to the size of the whole building. Where Palladio's villas have

[36] See pp. 30–35 above.

rooms laid out in harmonic relationships, the systematic dimensions may make it easier to carry a controlled scale treatment from room to room, and from a room to the whole interior. Underlying the geometrical scheme of harmonic systems is a search for firmer relationships between the parts and between parts and the whole. And while this objective may have originally appeared desirable because of classical conceptions of beauty or unity, it is also useful in the control of an observer's impressions of size.

The same value to design by human scale – a proportional system that firmly relates parts to larger wholes – accrues to Le Corbusier's Modulor. And when the basic module is frequently used, as he apparently intends it to be, it has the extra value of implanting a size that has been made familiar through frequent use. It is interesting to see the measures that were taken in the Marsailles Unité d'Habitation to expand the small modular unit to a ladder of sizes. The seventeen-story main block alternates large divisions (representing the two-story living rooms) and normal floors; and half way up, the big block is divided into two by a band of three ordinary floors. The interuptions of the shopping floor, and the elevator shafts and exit stairs, further help to spread the influence of the small measuring unit to the whole immense block. This, and the textural treatment of the concrete surfaces, is so expertly done that one must conclude that the large exterior scale of the design is a choice, 'by eye'; and we may further conclude that it properly expresses our attitude toward a community of this size under one roof.

When we disregard the claims that proportional systems create inherently beautiful shapes and relationships, or that they are precise in a mathematical-visual sense, we may allow that they make two contributions to designing in human scale. By their nature, they furnish systems of shapes that link part to part, and part to whole, in an orderly way. Where this order can be seen, it may be used to make a standard of measure firm, and to spread the influence of recognizable sizes throughout a design. In addition, proportional systems may stimulate the architect toward a more complete awareness of the interdependence of the parts of the building where they are not seen at the same time, or where they are seen together but not composed together. And in human scale, where the architect designs for the continuous experience of a spectator who moves within and around a building at will, these relationships are of the greatest importance.

It must not be supposed, because proportional systems may be

151

helpful in designing in human scale, that they are necessary to it. Modules may help to control the interiors and exteriors of Japanese houses in the way that is suited to designing for human scale. But Japanese gardens, without the benefit of modules, provide an even more skilful example of the control of a spectator's impressions of size. Similarly, if a harmonic proportional system helped Palladio to arrive at scale treatments that we find well regulated, the same measure of control is discovered in Baroque buildings and gardens where the system is of little importance. Le Corbusier has anticipated this kind of a comparison of his own buildings, by pointing out that his earlier designs were based upon 'regulating lines', and by asserting that the artist may intuitively arrive at the results that are more easily achieved with the Modulor. But he makes it clear, in any case, that his system is intended to be the servant, not the master, of the eye.

In the design of a single building, the practical way of building tends to provide the raw materials for human scale; and the proportional system tends to supply a useful part to part, part to whole, relationship. But in the design of many buildings – or of buildings in general – additional factors affect the relationship between human scale, physical measure, and proportional systems. Building materials, in our time, are supplied by sizable industries; and the building materials that the architect uses are normally chosen, not only because they are the best for a design, but also because they are economically manufactured in large quantities. Because of this, the relationship between human scale and physical measure extends beyond a single building's design and includes the method of construction – and the related treatment of scale – that will best harness the huge apparatus of the building industries. The architect discovers the relationship when he searches the catalogues for building materials that are available at reasonable prices. And in anticipation of the times, many architects have clearly seen that they must either demand desirable mass-produced components, or they will have to use undesirable ones.

This is not the place to examine the complicated patterns that distinguish a way of building – and a treatment of scale – for a single building, from a way of building for many buildings – and the corresponding treatments of scale. It suffices to observe that a treatment of scale is normally developed from the practical design synthesis that the architect has found for an economical use of materials, an efficient structural system, and a useful disposition of space. And in a highly industrialized society, this practical way of building is more and more determined by materials and services offered at a grand scale, and less and less often by those that are custom tailored to the individual building. No doubt, there will always be large, or important, structures for which it is reasonable to ask that industry re-tool its plants to make unique parts, or that workmen be especially trained. But for the great bulk of building, the desirable and practical pattern is more complicated. The architect, on the one hand, seeks to secure the highest standards of performance that can be got from industry, and on the other hand he must base his designs upon industry's offerings. His interest in ways of building, and in the scale treatment of them, cannot intelligently be confined to specific building designs. It must extend to whole classes of buildings that share the same technology.

Under the circumstances, the usefulness of a proportional system in the design of a single building is not a full indication of its value. The harmonic systems, which take their units from a base length's division into fractions, are at a serious disadvantage. They require units that are unique to the design of each project; and these are not likely to be easily, or economically, supplied by industry. Also, they tend to focus the designer's attention upon the internal relationships of a building and away from the relationships of a building to the open spaces around it or to other buildings. It is almost ironic that the relating of parts to larger parts, in the same manner that the larger parts are related to the whole – which makes harmonic proportional systems potent – should make the divisions ill-suited to mass production, and make it easy for the architect to conceive of the building as an isolated system of shapes. This order of relationship may be entirely appropriate to the design of villas in the open landscape; and it may not be a serious disadvantage in the design of churches or monuments that properly tower over and dominate their surroundings. But it is the very opposite of what is needed to solve our most pressing problems of design.

An absence of order in the streets, squares, and intervals between buildings is making the huge urban concentrations, in which we are increasingly to live, unfit for habitation by thinking and feeling people. Moreover, we have discovered how to perceive our surroundings so that a building is not only seen as an entity but is also seen within its context of open spaces and neighbouring buildings. Except for the 'throwbacks' among us, whose percep-

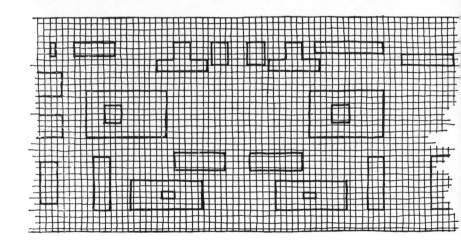

A grand interval which is recognized and understood

tion is naturally primitive, it does not seem possible to deliberately
espouse a proportional system that encourages the more limited
view.

To be fair, there does not seem to be any theoretical reason why
harmonic proportions systems cannot be applied to large building
complexes, and to the open spaces within them – using the over-
all dimensions of the project as the base length that is divided into
fractions. It is clear, however, that such a design would then
endow the large group of buildings with the tight internal relationships, and the non-existent relations with the larger surroundings, that characterizes the system. And it seems certain that,
unless the buildings were remarkably simple and uniform in
shape, it would be almost impossibly difficult to select divisions
that are convenient factors and also visually distinct.

Modular systems are obviously better suited to the requirements of mass production; and they do not have the centripetal
effect of fractional units. A jungle-gym grid, applied to all that
the architect is asked to design, makes it easier for him to imagine
all of the relationships that must be planned in order to control
the observer's experience. It introduces into the design a grand
interval which, like the module of Mies' I. I. Tech. campus, is
recognized and understood by the spectator from any position
that he may choose between the buildings, and which follows him
even when he enters them. Running through the design, the

modular grid may be used as a basic measuring unit. Within the grid, the smaller divisions of the design may be modulated for precise control of the scale; and the larger units of whole building shapes and open squares may derive their final quality of size as multiples of the unit dimension.

We should notice that this use of a modular grid cannot be infinitely extended. As projects become larger in scope, the standard unit becomes less effective as a measure of whole buildings, and of the spaces between them. In the extreme case of a project encompassing several city blocks – where there are large buildings as well as small ones, large open spaces as well as small courts, and where buildings will be seen from great distances as well as from close up – several modular grids at different sizes will be needed. The problem of how to satisfactorily relate small dimensions to large ones, which is easily solved in simple modular structures, is reintroduced. And although the modular grid may be helpful, the bulk of the problems of scale will remain to be solved by other means.

Because Le Corbusier's system departs from the generating spiral of the golden section with the basic Modulor unit, it seems to share the advantages and disadvantages of modular systems in general. However, we have found that his system has additional interest for us, not so much because of the modular scales themselves, as because of the way that they have been presented. We have already observed that Le Corbusier wished to find a way to measure space, corresponding to the way that sound is measured by time and pitch in music. And we have noticed that the practical problem that led him to undertake a study of measuring units was the search for the most desirable standards for the manufacture of building materials. He makes it clear that the Modulor is intended to release the designer's imagination, not to confine it. The scales are intended to encourage him to see, and to anticipate, the dimensions and relationships that he selects for a design. And the basis that he chooses for the system is the geometrical series of the golden section which whirls, or multiplies, toward infinity with a breath-taking dynamism.

If we encountered the Modulor scale, saw the variety of shapes that it generates, but had no further evidence of the creator's conceptions, it would be necessary to conclude that – like other geometrical proportioning systems – it has values that are useful in designing but it is a somewhat abstract conception. Colours, shadows, qualities of illumination, and viewing angles and distances, all intervene between the geometrical purities, on paper, and their appearance as they are seen in a building. But Le Corbusier has made it clear that he values the Modulor because it helps him to imagine, and to precisely anticipate, the effects of shapes and the relationships between shapes, as they will be seen on the finished building by real spectators. All practical considerations aside, he shows that he values the system because it helps a designer to define precisely, and to divide, portions of a vast space continuum of all defined space – to design for a scaled world.

If we allow that, to a designer, one of the principal values of proportional systems is their ability to stimulate him to a greater comprehension of the relationships of design, the bases of the Modulor – if not its final form – make the relationship of a building to the larger world around it inescapable. It is intended to provide a tool that will add precision and assurance to the free creation of visual order in a real world; and the visual world is a continuum of space, to be divided and defined by architecture. This continuum may be related to other present-day concepts of space in some way that has not been made clear to me.[37] But its importance in architecture derives from its complementary relationship to a spectator's real-life experiencing of his surroundings.

The environment is experienced in a continuous fashion. The unit of size with the greatest integrity is not found in a building, in a marker, but in the length of a day. The continuity of impressions of size begins in memory, and even in the subconscious mind. But it is actively stimulated by the surroundings during the waking hours. In my own case, the reasonable unit of size is from about seven in the morning to eleven at night in Princeton, New Jersey. During this time, there are long periods of meaningless relationships with the surroundings that cause me to ignore them. But this is because my experience has been arbitrarily fragmented or cut off. It is not inherent in my way of living or seeing; and we have seen that this walling up of what should be a lively stimulation from the surroundings interferes with natural and rewarding relationships.

Of course, people do not normally spend all of their waking hours appreciating the environment with all of the intensity that they can muster. Attention is naturally turned inward from time to time; and much of the time it is divided between inner

[37] Siegfried Giedion, *Space, Time and Architecture*, Cambridge, Mass. 4th ed. 1962.

*The reasonable
unit of size*

preoccupations and the surroundings. But chaotic surroundings
are not the best setting for either the outer or the inner life. It is
when all is serene and ordered without, that the most profound
concentration within is made possible – as every Japanese moon
platform builder knows. The potential, and the ideal, continuity
of scale is one that controls and orders impressions of size throughout the day, wherever one ventures. An afternoon spent in a
Baroque garden – where all that is seen is planned and under
control; a day in a medieval city – where practical planning has
produced much the same results; or an hour in a fine building,
should serve to show that where there is no continuity of meaning
to be found the spectator is, in a sense, less alive. Le Corbusier's
vision of a city in which all relationships of size are brought into
harmony with the help of the Modulor, is the design counterpart
of the ultimate and natural demand for human experience.

In our time, the architect who learns to control relationships of
size in the exterior of a building, in its interior, and finally
wherever the spectator is able to experience his design, has his
attention inevitably led to the conception of a world that accommodates the continuity of sizes as they are experienced – from
awakening to sleeping, wherever the spectator is. The extension
naturally fits his conception of space as a continuum to be divided,
shaped and defined by design. And it matches to some extent the
practical problems of construction which, as we have seen, draw
his attention from the materials and construction of one building
toward a consideration of the materials and way of building cities,

or nations, of buildings. We may consider that Le Corbusier's Modulor, aside from its value as a measuring and proportional system, is important as an instrument that may help the architect to grasp wider relationships in design. And it is possible that its greatest value lies in the invitation, to conjure up a world of scale, that it extends to a lively imagination.

Our discussions of human scale have led to a similar departure. We have found that the norm of human scale varies with the observer's expectations; and we have discovered that large scale and small scale are design tools – with an eloquence all of their own – that can be used when the continuity of the observer's impressions of size is maintained. This, again, depends on his expectations; but we have seen that these are not solely preconceptions. From the architecture itself, what is before the eyes, and what persists in the memory, also determine his expectations. The treatment of a building's scale may control most of the observer's experience of sizes when he is within it, and much of it when he is out of doors. But once the essential continuity of his experience is grasped, attention is led to the larger site, to the city and to the world of size relationships – in which the building takes its place, and from which it draws its final qualities of size as they are experienced.

A World of Scale

It is inevitable that the idea of a world of scale, or some similar conception, should emerge from a discussion of human scale. As experienced visually, sizes are relative. Once the designer begins to explore their relationships within a building design, he cannot fail to observe that they are enmeshed with the sizes of other buildings, and with the sizes of the open spaces defined by them. And from this larger sphere of relationships, his attention is led further to encompass the entirety of the network of sizes that an observer may encounter.

Until now, we have been content merely to observe the indications of a modern world of scale as they have emerged in our discussions. What we have had to say about scale has not depended on them. Thus, we assumed that a useful description of human scale must be compatible with the modern architect's comprehensive approach to the design of space, but we did not explain exactly how human scale may be related to it. In the last chapter we did not follow up the suggestion that Le Corbusier's Modulor may represent the search for a world of scale to match his world of space. Nor did we immediately pursue the observation that contemporary physical, proportional, and human scale suggest an extension to the entire environment. Human scale is an entirely workable conception without the theoretically desirable connection with spatial designing, and it is reasonable and complete without being extended to the entire environment. But now that the distinction has been made clear, a simple relationship can be shown between human scale – as we have described it – and the definition of a continuum of space. And although the grand scheme of a modern world of scale must remain somewhat elusive, it can be shown that it is by no means the complete abstraction that the words may suggest.

Like most important discoveries, the visual design of archi-

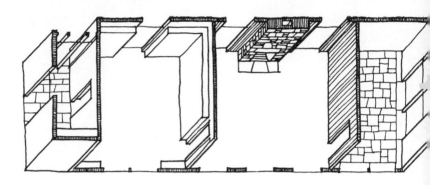

The views are most easily organized about four nuclei

tecture as a space continuum is essentially simple. We may easily examine most of its basic premises by comparing several of the ways that a series of connected rooms may be designed in order to control the experience of a spectator walking through them. No matter how they are designed, the observer will experience them as a continuous sequence in time, beginning when he enters the first room and ending when he leaves the last one. But in one design the sequence of his views may add up to little more than the sum of experience afforded by the separate rooms. In another, it may be planned to contribute a distinctive character of the whole sequence. Thus, when four rooms are merely juxtaposed – as they are in the period-room wing of a museum – the spectator will find it convenient to organize his experience about four clear unifying conceptions; and the final effect of his tour is likely to be no more than a recollection of the four conceptions. But when the rooms are designed so that each complements, or contrasts agreeably, with the others – as they will in any well-designed suite of rooms – he will experience the additional unifying conception of a harmonious suite. In either of these designs, the period rooms or the suite, the views that he continuously experiences throughout his explorations are most easily organized about four nuclei. They describe four distinct defined spaces.

But a spectator's visual experience does not have to be organized around room shapes, as it was in these two examples. His scope of vision includes whatever he can see: through doors and windows, indoors, and out of doors. From wherever he stands, it tends to integrate the visual elements that he can see into a unit that is incongruous with the division of the plan into rooms. Because of

160

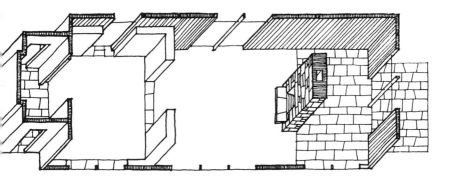

Four conceptions of volume that evolve each one into the others

this, the shapes, hues, and empty spaces of one architectural space, as often as not, are shared by other architectural spaces. And when a series of rooms are opened into one another, the spaces that are defined for the spectator's scope of vision are interdependent and overlapping in plan. This overlapping, and the continuous nature of the observer's experience, suggests that the entire suite of rooms may be designed so that it is not only seen in a continuous series of views as any design is, but it is also continuously joined in the observer's mental organization of what he sees.

This effect may be approximated in the design of a suite of rooms that open into each other. Many of the shapes, hues, and distances may be shared by several of the rooms; and the basic conceptions of volume – the nuclei of the observer's conceptions of defined space – may be overlapping conceptions. In a suite of rooms designed in this way, the observer's conception of one of the rooms has only to be modified or developed as he passes into the adjacent room. Consequently, his experience of the four rooms will be organized about four conceptions of volume that are not sharply differentiated but evolve, each one into the others.

From a suite of rooms linked in this fashion, it is only a short step to a design in which the idea of volume – the conception that the visual experience is organized around – is no longer identified with a physical enclosure or room. The suite may be so designed that as the spectator moves – and as the scope of his vision shifts to bring into view new shapes, colours and distances, – the volume that serves as the nucleus of his visual experience also moves and shifts. The sequence of views, organized in this manner, defines a continuum of architectural space which matches the

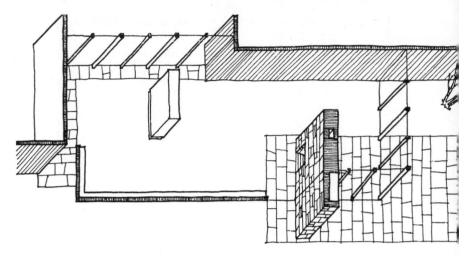

The conception of volume evolves continuously as he moves

continuity of the spectator's views throughout the design. Looking at the plan of this design, it may be impossible to distinguish the various architectural spaces. They are generated around any position that the observer may take; and they are so overlapping that, although the spectator is surrounded by a carefully composed defined space in any part of the design, the conception of volume that his views are organized about evolves continuously as he moves.

Obviously, this approach to designing is more than compatible with human scale as we have described it. Both human scale and the definition of a continuum of space have as their basis the observer's mode of perception and the way that he forms his impressions of size, in the one instance, and of defined space in the other. The only 'trick' for either the designer or the observer may be relinquishing an habitual, and deceptively simple, assumption that the compositional whole of a design must coincide with a whole physical division – with the whole block of a building or with the whole cell of a room. It is prudent to observe that where physical divisions and conceptual wholes do not coincide, the system of sizes that controls architectural scale must be planned with particular care. This caution applies to all of the elements of a design that are to be continuously joined and remembered by the observer, because the whole of the design will be the space that is defined by the views that can be continuously and cumulatively joined in the mind. But the treatment for scale – the ladder of sizes to make it easy to relate small parts to the whole design, and the control of the observer's standard of largeness or smallness – remains the same. Human scale, as we have developed it, may be applied without modification to the design of a space continuum.

Neither the design of architecture around a continuum of space, nor the scale treatment of it, is significant because it is a better way to design or because it is always a convenient way to work. They are important because they are comprehensive approaches to designing which embrace other, less inclusive, kinds of imagination. The designer who conceives of architectural space as a continuum has the free choice of all of the other kinds of conception that are more limited in their scope of application. Designing in architectural spaces, he may decide to make portions of his buildings flat and two-dimensionally conceived, or to make them sculpturally massive or cell-like in division. And he may decide to confine himself exclusively to the relationships of size in a block shape or in the divisions of an isolated room. But the choice of these less-inclusive approaches to designing space, or scale, may be made only after the entire range of experience that can be controlled has been brought to the designer's attention. Thus, the architect may elect to make two buildings, or two rooms, unrelated in treatment of either scale or space, but he is not allowed to overlook their relationships. The divorcement must be deliberate.

To define a continuum of space is to design with an all-embracing eye, for we have seen that the composition must include and control whatever may lie within the observer's scope of vision. This aspect of the continuum of space makes it the least arbitrary and the most directly sensuous approach to composition. It has been given a vivid exposition in the *Architectural Review*'s long series of 'Townscape' articles where the all-embracing eye gives to lamp posts, trash cans, traffic signs and paving stones the important place that they occupy in the observer's scope of vision. The attention to details may at time seem a little finicking. But the approach to design that focuses on these details is the same one that brings into one composition harbours, hills, clusters of fine old buildings and the sprawling networks of highways. The continuum of space logically includes these diverse phenomena in one composition. And because of this, it may be identified as the approach to designing that can govern what we have called a 'normal' unit of scale – a man's experience of sizes throughout a day, wherever he goes. Theoretically at least, the experience of a day can be designed as a continuum of space in which nearly all of the positive factors of scale are controlled, excluding only the expectations shaped by an observer's recollections of other days.

It is the expansive nature of the continuum of space that makes it necessary to look for a distinctively modern conception of the whole field of relationships of scale. When the scope of a continuum of defined space is not arbitrarily limited, as it was in our sequence of four rooms, it tends to suggest its own extension. Even in the design of a small house, for example, the area that must be considered relevant to the design includes all of the interior, the exterior, the grounds around the house, and the other buildings, streets, hills, church steeples, etc. that can be seen from the property. Following the scope of vision, the continuum naturally enlarges itself to include whatever may be seen from the area that the designer has been asked to arrange; and from this enlarged sphere, again, to draw the designer's attention to all that can be seen. In this way, it naturally leads him to assume that all space – the whole world if you please – is a continuum defined by related visual parts. Within it, the parts that he is designing are distinguished from the rest of the continuum primarily because he is able to control them.

The comprehensive nature of composition by continuum of space makes it expansive in scope. When a designer is composing a picture on a plane, his primary reference is the rectangular area within the frame. When he is composing either spaces that coincide with room divisions or masses that correspond to building-blocks shapes, these volumes and masses are the natural focus of his attention. But when he is designing architectural spaces that do not have to coincide with room shapes, which overlap and which may be composed about an evolving nucleus, there is no reason inherent in his method of composition why the design cannot be infinitely extended.

There is every evidence that even a small portion of this expanded scope of designing carries with it responsibilities that our most imaginative architects are poorly prepared to assume. With very few exceptions, contemporary designs for large groups of buildings are much more diagramatic than designs for individual buildings. As the projects increase in size, more and more of the work escapes the architect's firm imaginative control. We have learned to expect that projects the size of a 'super-block' or a 're-development area' shall have large portions that were incompletely imagined before they were built and are consequently barren in

164

their effect. Within them, the spectator feels as though he were walking through a grotesquely enlarged model and, like an insect, perceiving accidental shapes that are not noticed by the larger animals.

Our very large designs – plans for whole cities or regions – are usually as chillingly abstract when they are completed as they were in the programming stages of design. Some of the critics of urban design appear to believe that this deadly design vacuum is an inevitable consequence of large-scale planning. It should be recognized, rather, as a consequence of imperfect imagination. And although it arises from the large scope of the designs, it is not an inevitable, or even a normal, consequence of their size. The factual bases that underlie large-scale plans are often indisputable: the assignment of land uses, the determination of desirable population densities, the highway and street patterns, etc. We certainly should not be discouraged from boldly setting out to re-arrange our environment because of the deficiencies in our urban designs. Not planning is the infinitely worse alternative. But the tangible qualities of urban designs cannot stand comparison with the qualities of our fine buildings – they provide an X-ray world of strong theoretical bones and shadowy flesh. We may rejoice in the fact that most of our major architects, and many lesser ones, are designing large urban complexes, and even whole new cities. There is no other group of designers who are properly trained to undertake these projects. But at the same time, we must observe that there is a pressing need for an enlargement of the architect's field of imaginative conception in order to bring to life the area staked out by the expanded scope of his competence in spatial composition.

A way of imagining very large relationships of size is, of course, very much the crux of the matter. And this is why we have examined with special interest Le Corbusier's search for a suitable way to measure the world of architectural space – it is a direct attack on the problem. With his usual boldness, he has designed a proportional system that incorporates two infinitely extendible ideas of measure – the golden section series of divisions and the module of the human figure – to create scales of measure for his infinitely extendible world of space. In the abstract, the golden section sequence sweeps from zero to infinity with an unbroken regularity that promises to match the endless coils of the space continuum. The human figure, used as a module, implies a similarly appropriate measure of a limitless world.

The brave logic of this choice does not stand up under a closer inspection. We have already commented on the contrast between the golden section, unrestrained, and its use in Le Corbusier's Modulor, where it is confined to the subdivisions of the modular scale. And we must now observe that Le Corbusier's use of the human figure implies a limitless world of scale that, oddly enough, is not the same world of scale that is suggested by his building designs. The Modulor system, taken as a rule rather than as a convenience (against the advice of its originator) implies the simplest and the most inflexible use of a human module for all designs; and this is the infinitely expansible conception that can match the expanding scope of designing by space continuum. But the architectural works of Le Corbusier, and in particular his more recent works, show that he does not merely follow his modular scales but uses them to create the versatility of mature human scale as we have described it here – large scale, small scale, and dynamic variations of scale. Le Corbusier's adventure into the design of a proportional system helps to point out, and to clarify, the need for a new way to imagine the whole warp and woof of relationships of size. It serves, further, to emphasize the problem of scale treatment provoked by the expanding scope of designing in the definition of a continuum of space. But it does not provide us with a useful model for this form of imagination.

I believe that it is mature human scale, with varied and flexible powers of measure, that must accompany the design of the continuum of space. But before we can attempt to describe this complicated world of flexible and varied relationships, we must consider several aspects of contemporary architecture that are not directly concerned with space-definition but which, directly or indirectly, suggest models for the control of the scale of the entire environment. Simple human scale, for social rather than aesthetic reasons, has been widely accepted as the universal contemporary expression of scale. New factors of physical scale – changes in building technology, sheer size and rapid motion – have been taken to be indicative or a new urban scale. In each of these cases there is a new relationship of sizes which must be accommodated in any useful description of the larger field of scale.

The widespread, and rather careless, championing of simple human scale, and of the human figure as a module, is particularly confusing as these approaches afford many advantages which dissipate when they are applied to the conception of a large field of relationships. The selection of the human figure as a module

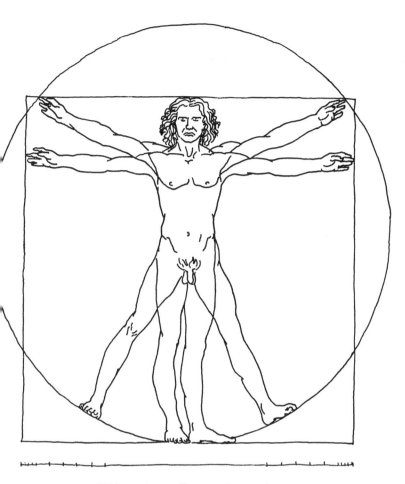

With various tributes to humanism

of size (usually with various tributes to humanism and to the Renaissance man) is symptomatic of a very significant contemporary attitude toward designing: it 'feels' somehow right. Simple human scale is often the best approach to the design of an individual building, and as we have remarked, it is a conception that can be extended to the entire environment. Nevertheless, these are singularly unsatisfactory and ineffectual models for a contemporary world of scale.

Human scale has been advanced with vague recommendations that it is socially desirable. Frank Lloyd Wright made human scale – his own very small version of it – one of the traits of his

167

'Usonian' architecture intended to represent accurately the rugged individualism of American democracy. Throughout the 'International School' ascendancy, human scale tended to be sentimentally equated with humanitarianism. In both of these instances, the choice of small or 'normal' scale appears to have been first suggested as a remedy for the frequently over-blown large scale of Beaux Arts architecture. But an additional parallel was assumed between the smaller-scale treatments and social progress. Large scale had been used for royal palaces and cathedrals, and human scale would represent the social order of the future. Walter Gropius, it is true, was interested in both the illusory experience of scale and in its variety; and he concluded that the architect should manipulate scale in order to further the purpose of his designs.[38] But the examples that he used illustrate the general bias in favour of small scale – large scale for temples and dictators' stadiums, small scale for a nursery school. André Lurçat fell into a somewhat different assumption. He equated human scale with the utilitarian and, because he supposed that the times were characterized by materialistic aspirations, he concluded that human scale afforded a logical basis for both domestic and collective programmes.[39]

The effects of human scale, when it is extended to all buildings – that is to say, to the whole field of relationships of size – are in direct contrast to the current of humanitarian sentiment that underlies these assumptions. In a sense, it is exactly the fact that simple human scale is one thing applied to isolated buildings, and another when applied to the whole environment, which has led us to develop a more flexible conception of scale. We found that the 'normal' appearance of the human figure, and the 'normal' relationship of the figure to buildings, changes from place to place, with the uses of the building and with ways of building.[40] And this necessary qualification of what is 'normal' reveals the complexity of what, at first, seemed to be a refreshingly simple conception of scale. If the measuring unit is to be extended to an infinite area, it either must continually vary in size in order to maintain a constantly 'normal' impression of size, or – kept to the standard module of the human figure – it will be variously interpreted according to the spectator's preconceptions of largeness and smallness.

[38] Gropius, op. cit.   [39] Lurcat, op. cit., p. 453.
[40] See pp. 79–88 above.

*Properly represent a thinking
and feeling individual*

In our development of a mature conception of human scale it seemed reasonable to suppose that a human scale that fluctuates with people's expectations should also allow the architect the full choice of planned variations in scale. By contrast, where the simple form of human scale moulds the visual world to a uniform module representing the human figure, is inherently restrictive. Its promise of simplicity, and its apparent affinity for what is humane, may be fulfilled only in the design of those individual buildings where the observer may be expected to interpret the module as 'normal'. Where it is applied to the entire environment, it restricts the architect to an arbitrarily inflexible module which will provide accidental variations in scale, and which cannot be manipulated to solve problems in the perception of size; in particular, it cannot be used to combat the tendency of large designs and vast dimensions to escape from sure measurement and to fluctuate by accident. Like most sentimental ideas, it is cruelly unrealistic in application. It ignores people's actual experience – their expectations of size, the heightening of experience through large and small scale, and the dynamic experience of variations in scale.

It is the sentiment that architectural scale should be somehow humane that shows us the valid observation underlying these careless assumptions. It is characteristic of our times that there is a new concern for the relative nature of designing. We are less concerned with the expression of absolute values and conventional symbols than was usual throughout the past, and we have been made increasingly aware that the values of a design are relative to the experience of the individual observer. This attitude should, of course, be as typical of our treatment of scale as it is of designing in general. But the assumption that it calls for the application of a uniform human-size module is mistaken. The mistake, essentially, is the assumption that the imprint of his height, repeated over and over again, properly represents a thinking and feeling individual. The proper and effective expression of this attitude is found in the contemporary architect's basic approach to spatial composition, which is 'observer centred', and in the treatment of scale appropriate to this mode of designing. A building, or a city, is – without sentimentality – humane when it is designed for the observer as he is found and as he perceives his environment. This is the approach to designing that has largely determined our development of a mature conception of variable human scale. And this is the attitude toward designing that must typify any useful model of a contemporary world of scale.

A number of contemporary factors have combined to make radical changes in the physical scale of architecture. Changes in building technology – which exert influences toward uniformity of parts – the sheer size and extent of urban construction, and the stepped-up speed of transportation, must be taken into account in the formulation of any useful conception of the whole field of visual scale. Of these changes, building technology exerts the most modest influence and is a widely misunderstood influence on architectural scale.

We have discussed the effects of modern industrial production of building parts upon the physical scale of architecture and upon the value of proportional systems in our time. Uniformity of shapes and dimensions is characteristic of the products and of the means of construction. The general level of design must be raised

Successful for the smaller buildings

by the efficient and excellent design of building parts that – to be inexpensive – must be widely used in many buildings. These realities have influenced most modern buildings; and where the architects have been acutely aware of the intimate relationship between physical and visual scale, they have often had an inhibiting influence on the treatment of scale.

The most distinguished illustrations of this chain of relationships – from uniformity of materials and structure to physical scale, and to visual scale – is undoubtedly found in the American designs of Mies Van de Rohe. Both his Illinois Institute of Technology buildings and his Lake Shore apartment buildings propose a polished architecture in which variations in scale are confined to the subtle arrangement of fine details. The main divisions of the

171

designs follow the module of the structural system and the window, door and wall panels. As in other tight syntheses between the practical and the visual, it seems quite possible that these divisions were partly determined by visual criteria. But it is clear that the method of construction is intended to dominate and to govern the visual design. Skilful control of the scale of these buildings is exerted through the austere arrangement of the necessary elements and, more interestingly, through the relatively free arrangement of elaborate corner and connection details of metal angles. Other projects, for example the Convention Hall for Chicago, indicate that a larger scale may be permitted for buildings of collective use with special long-span structural systems. But it is notable that even in the huge interior of the Convention Hall considerable effort has been made to reduce the scale as nearly as possible to that of the laboratory and apartment buildings.

In all of these buildings, the visual design closely follows the structural system, and the visual treatment of scale is confined to the slight manipulation that can be achieved by shaping and placing small details. The treatment is successful for the smaller buildings – the I.I.T. laboratories, for example. In the larger buildings, the wide gap between the over-all shape and the small details is so great that the impressions of size are not very securely controlled. The extent of this loss of control may be gauged on dark days when the illuminated ceiling planes supply the missing categories of large subdivisions.

The reasons that Mies gives for his approach to designing, in which the visual design is inhibited to support and to explain the structural arrangement, typify a common attitude toward building technology which is tenable applied to individual buildings but inadequate when applied to the whole environment. He supposes that architecture must be designed for the epoch rather than for the day; and he postulates that because we are living in an age of science and technology, we must accept building technology as the chief determinant of design – whether we like it or not. He has indicated that he believes architects should be looking for a vocabulary of building, rather than attempting to design masterpieces. And he has put forward the questionable argument that the 'prose' of architecture, done well enough, may become the poetry.[41]

[41] Mies Van der Rohe (and others), *Conversations Concerning the Future of Architecture*, phonograph record, side two. Ed. John Peter, Reynolds Metals Co., Louisville, Ky., 1956.

Now we cannot quarrel with these ideas if, as in the case of Mies, they have supported distinguished building designs. But we must observe the implications of this position when it is extended to the whole field of relationships of scale. Under the conditions of modern technology, a city composed of buildings that receive their major divisions from an efficient method of construction would present a monotony that could be of little use to an observer seeking to organize visually a neighbourhood or a community. Building technology simply cannot be depended on to supply, unaided, the modulations of size and scale needed to make a very large composition intelligible.

To judge from the variety of Mies' designs, this is not what he intends. Rather, he seems to visualize a city in which the bulk of ordinary buildings have this kind of a scale treatment, and the open spaces and infrequent public monuments are given different, and even contrasting, treatments. This is essentially a variation of the Baroque solution to the problem, which we shall discuss at some length below.

The value of the technical attitude toward designing for scale lies in the lesson that it conveys about the close connection between the physical and visual syntheses of architecture. Our large cities and huge buildings require a firm order if they are to escape visual chaos through meaningless differentiation; and the structural modules furnish one of the soundest bases for such an order. But in looking for a wider conception of scale we cannot afford, on the one hand, to consider human emotions and desires as ephemeral – to be ignored or even suppressed – while, on the other hand, we regard technology as a reality to be exclusively followed. This is an acquiescence to the material, and a proper discipline carried to the point of relinquishing what need not be given up. It may be as crippling for an architect of a different temperament as it is rewarding for Mies.

To suppose that technology can directly shape architecture shows a misunderstanding of the architect's function as an artist -- which is to discover a way to shape the physical world into an environment suitable for people as they are found. And it also ignores the vast wealth of materials and skills that technology has placed at his disposal. There is no inherent reason why the most modern materials, the most advanced structural techniques, and the most practical synthesis of them, should not furnish ample bases for the wide variety of treatments of scale that is needed to make our vast urban environment coherent. In the conception of

Dwarf modest buildings and intrude upon large ones

a modern world of scale, the uniform parts of modern technology supply a simplifying factor: we must make use of these materials.

The unprepared visitor to an urban planning exhibition is almost certain to be impressed by the insane size of the projects. The scope of the plans, and the size of the proposed buildings, hardly relates to his experience of existing cities; and he may easily suppose that the projects represent a sort of planner's day-dreaming. But it is not mere fantasy or an appetite for grandeur that has inflated the paper designs. The increased sizes are the results of powerful physical forces at work in the urban scene, and there is every reason to suppose that urban designers need to study and to practice designing on this expanded scale.

The most conspicuous generators of large sizes are the structures required for modern transportation. The runways for big aeroplanes are huge scars that cannot be assimilated into the suburban landscape. The multiple lanes, elevated roadways, and traffic pretzels of modern highways create a similar violent rip in the fabric of urban scale. The 'new scale' of these structures has two dimensions; speed and size. By their sheer size the highways dwarf modest buildings and topographical features, and they conspicuously intrude into the visual context of large ones. But because they are designed for speed, their large size and large scale are largely a consequence of the facts of transportation: easy curves, freedom from distracting details, and detachment from the clutter of smaller and slower streets.

Obviously, the disruption of the urban scale is not to be solved by reducing the scale of these new elements. They are scaled to their use and, whether they are used to convey people and goods through built-up areas or through the countryside, they provide the speed lanes with an appropriate visual statement. The problems of scale that they provoke must primarily be solved by their placement, rather than by tinkering with the details of bridges and roadways. They *should* introduce a jump in scale; but the break in the visual context can, to a great extent, be cushioned by our expectations and 'grounded' by our understanding of their function.

Placement calls for sure aesthetic and practical judgment; and even then, it can be counted on to raise perplexing problems. But satisfactory solutions seem to require an extension, not a replacement, of our ordinary bases for judgment. In the most confused of our cities, there are places where all of the parts – highways and their surroundings – fall into their proper relationship by accident or by design. In the country, there are hundreds of miles of divided highways that gracefully sweep around the contours – recognizing only the large features of the landscape – and enjoy an altogether agreeable relationship to the pastoral scene. Expressing clearly their function to collect and convey rapid movement, they run lightly across the fields, streams and woods, leaving them undefiled. It only remains for the poets to write as nostalgically about the hum of rural traffic as they have written about the distant hoot of the locomotive.

In town, the solution of the problem of the scale of highway construction does not appear to depart substantially from the proper and reasonable solution of land use, traffic and parking problems. Any of the practical schemes that have been proposed suggests a workable start for the treatment of scale. Where high-

It remains only for the poets to write as nostalgically

ways are to run grandly into the centre of town and terminate in parking towers, for example, the large scale elements may be made to contribute an eloquent dialogue with the centre of the city and with the smaller-scaled areas surrounding it. Where a town is designed in great 'superblocks' – each block surrounded by walls of fast moving traffic and turned inward toward its central pedestrian spaces – the arrangement may provide an equally satisfying basis for a treatment of visual scale. Both the arterial streets and the buildings that line them provide a large-scale frame for the soft interior of the block. And between this perimeter and the pedestrian cores there is room for a full range of scale treatment.

In town or in the country, the highway itself may provide the solution to some of the problems that it creates. The design may seek to show the traffic speeds; and the transition in scale, from large to small, may everywhere follow the pattern of speed, from fast to slow. Wherever it puts down a foot in the city, there is an opportunity for the highway to send out tentacles that are sensitive to the local topography and bind the highway into its smaller scales and slower traffic.

The present horrifying rents in the fabric of our cities are primarily the consequence of a one-way pressure of highways eating through feeble blocks of old buildings and accidentally creating sites for new ones. The sight horrifies and surprises for the same reason that it is terrifying to learn that some of us still practice cannibalism: it shows that we are capable of a crude fragmented vision that we thought we had left behind us in the course of evolution.

The size and large scale of our highways is not the only striking hiatus in the urban scene. Every year there are new buildings which, for their great size if for no additional reason, must appear isolated from the neighbouring buildings. In some instances the size of these behemoths is clearly the result of economic pressures – crowding more tenants into a high-rent district. But even where crowding does not force buildings into greater and greater concentrations, we may expect that logical planning will cause their size and scale to steadily increase.

Usually, when architects are allowed to plan an area of several blocks' extent, they find that the clients' requirements are more efficiently met through large buildings. Large regular structures, erected in a single building operation, are normally more economical. And large bold plans to control the organization of an entire area usually provide great advantages in the arrangement of common functions. For example, open spaces may be placed where they provide more light and air, and open finer views for all of the interior spaces. Traffic, parking, and convenient access, may be arranged for more of the tenants. And the centralized organization of pedestrian circulation may usually be made pleasanter and safer – separated from motor traffic – and at the same time more profitable commercially. The advantages are roughly analogous to those of the shopping centre over a casual aggregation of stores. Planning the relationships of the stores to each other, so that each receives the maximum benefit from its neighbours, and designing for parking and delivery service, usually results in an increase in convenience for the customers, an enhanced profit for the store owners, and a more uniform cheaper construction.

The size of buildings designed for a project of several blocks' extent is usually conspicuous. The row of similar office towers in the new central area of Stockholm is a striking landmark. The new buildings of Philadelphia's Penn Center are relatively large and stand out in the large spaces around them. But the full size, and a full measure of the bold designing encouraged by area planning, is revealed only when the entire project is considered. In both of these urban centres the tall buildings are joined at the ground level, or below grade, into what is essentially a single huge structure designed to provide the most advantageous arrangement of parking and transportation, and to facilitate the movement of large groups of people and the commercial exploitation of the circulation routes.[42] In this country, where the size of executed projects is likely to be established by the federal renewal programme, urban complexes of this kind may comprise several blocks of the central area of a town. And it has been made abundantly clear that in most instances the use of a few large buildings, rather than many small ones, frees the land for a superior over-all arrangement. Whenever capital is made available in the large amounts required, or whenever a city exercises intelligent control over the use of its land, we may expect larger buildings, larger spaces between them, and a new class of large visual dimensions. The enlargement – present and projected – is a new urban physical scale and to some extent it is an enlarged visual scale as well. This is partly, but not entirely, because of the close connection between physical and visual scale.

As we have observed in our discussions of scale and carrying-power, large buildings exert a pressure toward large-scale treatment. Shapes that are sufficiently large and emphatic to control an observer's experience of sizes at a considerable distance, tend toward large scale. The technical influences on physical scale – large sizes and their large scale, speed, and uniformity – have been repeatedly called to our attention in a confusing manner: as though the 'new scale' were somehow a model solution for designing. The new urban scale is a fact; the problems of scale that it provokes must be solved if architectural designs are to fit into the urban scene. And the solutions may be expected, at many points, to dictate the specific shapes and arrangements of a design. But large size, large scale, and uniformity are not visual characteristics that, stamped over a city, provide a satisfactory model for design-

---

[42] This is particularly true of the earlier scheme for the Penn Center, designed before financial difficulties caused the project to be revised.

ing. The individual, his mode of perception, and the structures designed for his intimate use, remain essentially unchanged. The new physical scale merely widens the gap between an observer's personal and direct experience of sizes, close to him, and his grasp of designs as intelligible wholes – one of the central problems of human scale.

For normal architectural projects, and even for designs encompassing several city blocks, the new problems of scale are most easily understood as aggravations of the familiar ones. A way must be found to link the intimate small-scale experience of a man walking on the sidewalk, sitting in a park, or standing in his living room, with dimensions of several blocks' length and of many stories' height. If his perception of sizes is to be easy and reliable, the scope of treatment for scale must be greatly expanded, while the intimate familiar problems of scale must still be solved.

Additional care must be taken to express the meaning inherent in buildings; what is inside them, how one should think of them, or how feel about them. The extra-large buildings in our vastly expanded cities seldom achieve a satisfactory treatment of scale by merely revealing their physical scale by accident (as many smaller structures do). More than ever before, the architect needs all of the versatility at his command – large scale, small scale, variations in scale, and the linking of scale with other forms of meaning.

If the full repertory of existing treatments of scale is needed to design adequately a project encompassing several blocks, something more is required to relate units of this size to other projects of the same scope, or to establish an intelligible relationship with the even larger elements that are inevitably drawn into the design of a continuum of defined space – whole cities, or the highways, hills and landmarks of a region. We have found that the new scope of design for scale is an extension to the entire environment. And although we have observed a recurring pattern of interest in it, and examined practical and theoretical considerations that favour its existence, this world of scale must remain speculative for the present. It does not exist in the unqualified example of an existing city.

The redevelopment of cities in the United States has provided only tantalizing hints of an over-all treatment of scale appropriate to the 'new urban scale'. The circumstances of rapid change and the relative immaturity of the urban designing profession, have lent to most of the work a quality of improvization and piecemeal planning that tends to limit the treatment of scale to the scope of projects that are seldom larger than two or four blocks. The new residential towns that have been built in Sweden and in England are not exceptionally large by contemporary standards, and they escape many of the pressures that might force a consciously expanded scope of treatment. Furthermore, where several different architectural firms have participated in the designs, there has tended to be a contrasting degree of control at practical and aesthetic levels – firm control of economic and physical factors, and much looser control of the co-ordination of visual designs.

The new cities that have been controlled from their foundations by able architects might be expected to supply the exception to the rule. At Brasilia an unusually vigorous attempt has been made to co-ordinate the parts of the visual design of an entirely new city. There is a studied relationship between buildings, open spaces, and traffic structures and a bold placing of the entire city in the wide open site. But if one can trust the published plans and photographs, the executed designs everywhere show signs of a hasty enlargement from model-size studies; and, as might be expected of an unfinished project, the treatment of scale in the spaces between buildings is one of the weakest aspects of the design.

There is a similar firm control of the visual design at Chandigarh under the leadership of Le Corbusier. In this instance the treatment of scale appears to have kept pace with the quality of the building designs in general. But the over-all scheme for scale is very similar to that of a Baroque city; and, for a provincial capital of its size, this may be an appropriate solution. The influence of the Baroque formula is more literally impressed upon Perret's reconstruction of le Havre, on the surprisingly Perret-like projects for Warsaw, and – with the peculiarly Russian value on vast open spaces – in the grand schemes for Moscow.

For lack of an existing design that attempts to treat the new bold scope of scale, we must construct our own model from the fragmentary traits that we have been able to observe. We cannot expect, in this way, to conjure up the vision of a new framework of relationships of size in space. But we may hope to trace some of its inevitable salient features and, more important, to discover the direction that promises a measure of success in the solution of contemporary problems.

It is only to be expected, after all, that a conception as abstract as a treatment of scale for the space continuum should precede significant attempts to apply its all-embracing influence to city planning. And it is not remarkable that the nature of the conception should be so clearly suggested in spatially designed buildings, while larger realizations remain only sketchily indicative of it. In another era, the germ of conception might have been a simple geometrical conception of order – such as the Hellenistic block planning idea, or the geometry underlying the Renaissance 'ideal cities'. Yet even these influential, but relatively uncomplicated, ideas were slow to emerge in executed designs. Hellenistic town plans in which the squares and monuments fully exploit the visual advantages of the grid street system are rare and late. The geometry of the 'ideal cities' found its way into circular church buildings long before it influenced city plans. What eludes us now is the vivid imagination of a complete continuum of scale, vested in imagined shapes and bathed in imagined sunlight. What we have been able to establish is a number of the specifications that it must meet if it is to be useful in our times.

The Baroque Model

Because of the disembodied nature of what we are seeking, it is helpful to examine an old model for an environment in which each characteristic treatment of scale is illustrated by actual buildings, squares and streets. The clearest model is, of course, the Baroque conception. It is archaic, with serious flaws; yet it is based on the realities of perception and – in its own peculiar way – linked to the social and economic life of the times. Indeed, it still has its apologists who, as the heirs to the City Beautiful Movement, have often been the butt of scornful jibes by more advanced urbanists. The scorn may be justified because of the obvious foolishness of trying to shape new cities with the mould of old ones. But the Baroque model provides an example that is unmatched in one respect. There is no other regulating model that as lucidly controls the visual design and the scale of as large an area.

The Baroque treatment of urban spaces is a logical development from the design of buildings. The architects were very much interested in organizing masses to provide effects of recession and movement as a building was viewed from different directions and distances. Thoroughly aware of the effects of their designs as views – analogous to theatrical scenes – they consciously exploited the open spaces around buildings as foreground, setting, and foil, for the masses of the structure. In many designs these preferences found expression in pavilions and porticos with a slight projection that only suggest movement and freedom from the main block of the building. But in large designs, where the architect was free from restraint, wings were extended to actually capture the adjacent open space, or buildings were ranged entirely around the space. As the observer changed his viewpoint, the masses of the building were alternately foreground or background, centres of interest or settings; and the open spaces between them were thoroughly integrated into the design. Consequently, the archi-

Aware of the effects of their designs as views

tect had at his disposal an urban design vocabulary of squares, circles and streets in which the masses and spaces were thoroughly imagined and understood in a relationship of interdependence. And the skills that enabled him to exploit the open spaces around a building were applied to the composition of sequences of squares and streets. They might be hollowed out of existing cities, or they might be laid out in independent new geometrical arrangements; but they were always designed with an eye to the pictorial effects available to a free observer.

The Baroque approach to the design of urban spaces continued,

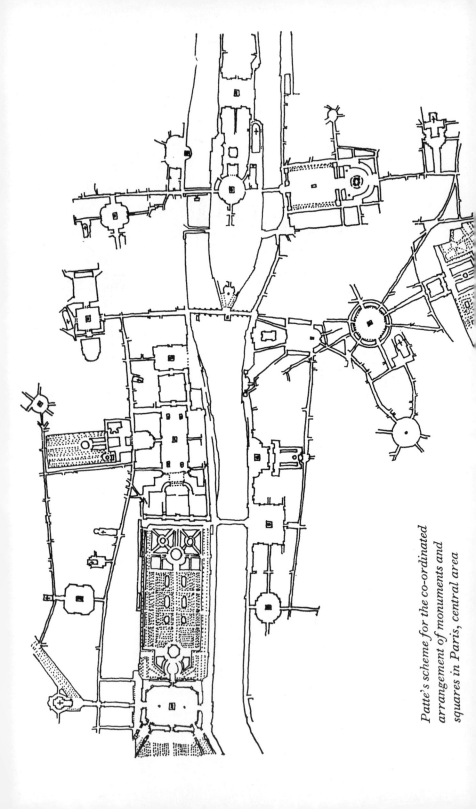

*Patte's scheme for the co-ordinated
arrangement of monuments and
squares in Paris, central area*

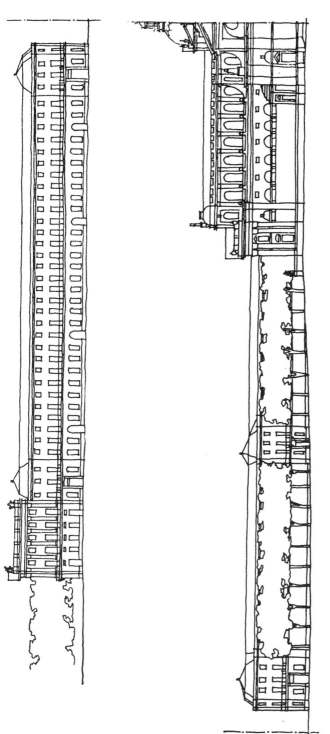

Design for the Rue Royale and the Madeleine suggested by Patte's engravings

essentially unchanged, through the subsequent stylistic evolutions to the Rococo and the Classical Revivals. In the eighteenth century it was enriched by a rational, but odd, concern for suitability to function. In the late nineteenth century it became difficult to apply, for a number of reasons that we shall discuss later. Nevertheless, it continued to be the major urban planning tradition of the Beaux Arts period of eclecticism. And in spite of the long time elapsed, we may consider Patte's plan for the co-ordinated arrangement of monuments and squares in Paris an application of the Baroque conception,[43] and we may regard Haussmann's rebuilding of the central part of Paris as an attempt to apply it – nearly always suffering from inflation – to a large city plan.

As an all-embracing co-ordinating system for the treatment of scale within a city, the mature Baroque system may be briefly summarized. It is assumed that there is a scale appropriate to the use of a building. Really small, domestic scale is reserved for small houses in the country, intimate interiors, and for some garden and street furniture. A moderately large scale, roughly appropriate to the street width, is considered proper for truly urban structures of a purely private residential or commercial use. And definitely large, but not gigantic, scale is reserved for public monuments such as churches, palaces, markets and exchanges.

With this hierarchy in mind, a city may be imagined as a layout of streets, lined with moderately large-scale private edifices – approximately the scale suited to the viewing distances of the street widths – which terminate at squares or monuments that may present a larger scale. A smaller scale may be used for interiors according to the use of a room – a closet, chamber, salon, or great hall. And the major monuments of the town, placed so as to dominate the streets, the squares, and the skyline, are in a large scale commensurate with their importance. The basic scheme is firmly established by major design elements – the building block shape, roof shapes, cornices, large orders, and arcades. And within this framework, small-scale sequences and small-scale framing provide variety and dynamic interest outside and inside the buildings.

There are a number of designs composed of several streets and squares which show that the system is effective. The famous squares at Nancy or Copenhagen, for example, illustrate the firm control of the norm of largeness-smallness that is established, and

[43] Pierre Patte, *Monumens Erigés en France*, Paris, 1767.

Reserved for public monuments　　　　　*Proper for truly urban structures*

the subtle treatment of scale that is possible within the framework. It is equally clear from the Louis XV schemes for Paris (and from the additional evidence of the squares that were actually executed) that the system is effective for a small city with streets that are not excessively long and buildings that are not too varied in character. The treatment of scale is so simple that it is immediately grasped and it clearly relates to the uses of the buildings in broad general categories. A normal urban scale is firmly established and large-scale or small-scale departures from it are used to make the nature of the buildings and open spaces intelligible. The dominant placing of public buildings is appropriate to their large-scale treatment; and the scale, in turn, is suited to the longer distances from which they will be seen. The shorter viewing distances and the smaller scale of private buildings are equally well matched.

187

But the most impressive product of the Baroque treatment of scale may be the well-founded assurance that it gave to the architects. Mistakes in judgment were made, and infrequently wilful rifts were made in the system. But there was a common understanding of a whole environment of scale. And even in ordinary building designs, where the architects were not able to control elaborate masses or considerable ranges of distance, this usually imparted a sure serene skill in the treatment of sizes. Whether the standard of size was carried to the edge of the site by adjacent buildings, or carried only in the imagination, it contributed order and coherence to the design.

There is also a satisfactory solution to the problems of scale that are provoked by people's having different standards of largeness-smallness in different places. By fortuitous circumstances rather than by design, the Baroque system makes it possible to vary the norm of scale from city to city in order to accommodate local circumstances or to reflect broad cultural differences; and this is accomplished without creating a damaging break in experience. The reason for this was observed by Georges Gromort who – as a Beaux Arts heir to the tradition – recast many of its premises in the light of modern insights and gave some thought to this problem. He observed that because a building in a city is seldom isolated from other buildings, the true scale is recalled by neighbouring structures. When there are none – as when driving through a landscaped park – the image remains. But if we stay isolated from these reminders the memory goes away after a period of time.[44] The standard of largeness-smallness (true scale) is a memory that, in a city, is normally refreshed and regenerated by the sight of the buildings. Without this stimulus it can be sustained for a limited period of time.

The Baroque system provides a norm of scale throughout a city. The variations from the norm, adjusted to the use of buildings and open spaces, are those the observer expects to see; and they do not interfere with the sense of reality established by the standard of size. The same norm, with the same kind of adjustments for suitability, is maintained in the monuments, chateaux, gardens and road allées of the environs of a city. But as one approaches the country the landscape becomes more and more filled with trees and gardens, and the standard of size is eventually supplanted by the physical scale of farms and forest preserves. In this environ-

[44] Gromort, op. cit.

188

ment, memory may be relied upon to sustain a standard of size across a park, or even from chateau to neighbouring chateau, but it cannot be expected to persist for the greater distances from city to city. Consequently each city – as a relatively small island in the countryside – may have its own true scale that is adjusted to local conditions; and each significant difference in culture may be reflected in the norm of size. The differences between standards of size are absorbed by the 'cushion' of the countryside. The use of this buffer, furthermore, is not inconsistent with the architect's distinction between art and nature. Wherever the design is consciously contrived, in town or country, the scale is controlled by a consistent standard. And it is only in the rustic countryside – the landscape of nature rather than of art – that it escapes from control.

The clarifying effects of the Baroque system of order between buildings and open spaces, may be observed in the streets and squares that have been left to us. And we may reconstruct an additional order, between city and city and between city and surrounding country, from eighteenth-century maps and prints. At Versailles, for example, there is a scale sequence – from the great square facing the palace, to a grand axial street, to tree-lined roads, to the farmland, – in which the standard of size is not so much altered as gradually supplanted by the countryside's 'nature'. Approaching Paris from Versailles, the sequence is experienced in reverse – farmlands, chateaux and gardens, city gates, and formal city streets and squares.

If the scale of Versailles is not that of Paris (it is smaller) it is not likely to be carried in memory from Versailles to Paris. Each change in scale is suitably adjusted to the uses of a place and, at every point, the standard of size may be accepted without question as 'real'. For its time, this is a satisfactory plan for a world of scale embracing the entire environment.

In our time the limitations of the Baroque treatment of scale have become serious weaknesses. When it is extended to control the scale of a city of more-than-moderate size the means of control lose their power. Because it obtains its clarity from a simple heirarchy of spaces and scales, it is particularly suited to the expression of broad set contrasts of meaning, rather than intricate flexible gradations. Haussmann's Paris is only a fraction of present-day Paris, which is not one of our largest cities. Yet Second Empire Paris contains distances that make it impossible for the important monuments to maintain their function in the Baroque system of

The streets are made dreary and scaleless by extended openness

scale. At the ends of long avenues they are reduced to vague smudges easily lost among the vehicles. And the streets, deprived of their terminating climaxes, are made dreary and scaleless by extended openness. Where old Baroque buildings have had new areas opened around them, comparison with the sizes of the new streets and squares makes them unimpressive; and the shapes designed to read from modest distances are often unintelligible. Where the architects were required to design new buildings for the inflated street spaces, they were faced with a scale problem that could not be solved within the Baroque formula. If they designed the new structures in a scale suitable to their use and importance, the structure's influence was too feeble to control the long distances and wide open spaces of the new city. If they increased the scale and carrying power of the shapes in order to match the longer viewing distances, the designs tended to be crude and overbearing seen close up and to be pretentious out of all keeping with their function.

A similar problem of scale and distance may be observed in the palace at Versailles which is, in this respect, an a-typical Baroque example. Expansion after expansion of the chateau and its gardens could not be accommodated through adjustments of the scale and carrying power of the architectural shapes. The basic vocabulary of shapes had been established in the earlier executed portions that were also the most important portions of the palace – the king's apartments. At Versailles the problem is partially solved by the way in which the gardens are brought up to the palace. On the main axis, most of the façade is screened from view by masses of trees, and in the remaining gap before the palace, a fountain reinforces the centre of interest. From the sides, attention is led to a climaxing open space before the chateau rather than to its façade.

In Second Empire Paris, the problem is inherent in the size of the city. Long avenues were needed for coherence and convenience, and it was often impossible for these spaces to interact with buildings in the Baroque manner. This may have been one of the factors contributing to two conspicuous traits of Beaux Arts architecture that have often been considered merely frivolous. The designs tend, on the one hand, to have the kind of wild exuberance that is seen in the Grand Palais or the Ponte Alexandre. And this may have been an attempt to make buildings dominate the large spaces through vigour and suggested movement. On the other hand, the designs tend to be given the exaggerated and inappropriate large-scale treatments that were so objectionable to the early architects of the Modern Movement. This second trait imparts a nightmare air of unreality to some of the buildings – for example the Brussels Palais de Justice or, in this country, the Philadelphia City Hall – but it does extend their sphere of influence over the surrounding spaces.

A particularly fascinating illustration of the scale-space problems that were encountered is provided by the step by step enlargement of the axis in Paris which begins at the Louvre, runs through Gabriel's Place de la Concorde, and terminates at Napoleon's huge arch. The last important additions to this composition were the rebuilding of the end pavilions of the Louvre (formerly parts of the Tuileries) in an over-blown scale, and the planting of trees behind the little arch of the Carrousel – an admission that the central façade of the palace cannot be made to relate to the new distances.

The diversity of modern urban life places another strain upon the Baroque system. The simple code of scale-to-use depends on sharp distinctions between public and private buildings, and between important buildings and lesser ones. When the attempt is made to record the subtle differences between modern hotels, apartment buildings, and department stores, or between private theatres, public auditoriums and school halls, it loses the coherence that is its very means of control. To fit the Baroque system, a large department store – for instance – would have to be given the importance and the scale of a palace or, equally unsatisfactory, sneaked behind a façade appropriate to several smaller functions. The bulk of a huge filing-cabinet office building simply refuses to be incorporated into the scheme because its size and importance cannot be equated. The very large size, the inevitable variety of activities to be housed, and the lack of correspondence between size and importance, cause the Baroque system to burst at the seams.

The regulating lines and masses in Haussmann's Paris forced an odd variety of functions behind inexpressive facades. In present-day Leningrad, Moscow, or Warsaw we may observe a similar 'dead-pan' expression for block after block of new buildings. Their varied functions have been suppressed – in a caricature of the Baroque system – in order to set off government bureaux or palaces of culture.

It may be supposed that the city-wide scheme that we have attributed to Mies would be smarter, neater, and more responsive to the different uses. Nevertheless, a city of monotonous physical scale punctuated by monuments must be pressed into a shape that does not conform to its activities. And it is clear that a modern city can be made to capture the clarity of a Baroque relationship between use and scale only at the excessive price of misrepresenting the variety and vitality of its social organism.

New circumstances have also invalidated the Baroque solution to the scale relationships between cities, and between town and country. The distances from the centre of our major cities to the open countryside, has steadily increased until now it is more often measured in hours than in minutes. Our cities are surrounded by a new class of structures that neither fit into the 'natural' farmlands nor belong in a truly urban order of buildings. The countryside itself has changed. It is no longer covered with a rustic carpet

*Imparts a
nightmare air
of unreality
to some*

Our cities are surrounded by a new class of structures

of farms and forests. Industrial and extracting operations are scattered throughout it; and, increasingly, agriculture is conducted on very large farms interspersed with marginal lands in various stages of neglect. Dr. Doxiadis, who has designed urban plans around the world, prophesies that the countryside will soon consist of islands of green within a continuous city.[45] Mr. Jean Gottman, who is making a study of the megalopolis that stretches along our East Coast, concludes that distinction between 'rural' and 'urban' will soon become obsolete.[46] And anyone may observe that each year the open country is less of a neutral cushion between cities. Under the conditions, it is impossible to apply the Baroque solution. The edge of town, where an urban scale may gradually be supplanted by the natural landscape, has become hard to find. And the buffer of neutral countryside, which may absorb changes in standards of size, is indecisive in character and shrinking.

But it is when we stand back and look at the entire Baroque system for controlling scale – within the cities and between them – that we discover its most serious limitation for our time. Its very backbone is the establishment of a single norm of size; and this standard governs wherever there is architecture – as opposed to nature, or to buildings that were looked upon as merely functional. To apply such a norm to an area the extent of a modern city – or worse, to an area the size of our chains of linked cities – is to inhibit the treatment of scale to a range that is becoming ineffectual. To make these large areas coherent, we need the full variety

[45] Public Lecture at Princeton, 1961.
[46] Jean Gottman, *Megalopolis: the Urbanized Northeastern Seaboard of the United States*, New York, 1961.

of scale treatment, including the controlled modulation of the standard of largeness-smallness itself.

These modulations may be used to provide a large structure of relationships that was not needed in the Baroque world. The cities were relatively small, and the uniform standard of size was usually relieved by accidental interruptions caused by the older buildings that remained, by functional buildings that were not treated as architecture, or by the intrusions of the countryside. The structure that may be created through modulations in the standard of size is analogous to the great skeleton of modulations in key that underlies the classical symphonic works. Its power to interpret the urban scene may be felt while driving through the successive 'growth rings' of most American cities – through the central business district, the apartment house belt, commercial ring, built up suburbs, and the green suburbs. The meaningless juxtaposition of standards of size that is encountered may be the most disruptive force in our unplanned cities. But where the modulations of the norm of size coincide with changes in visual and social character, they may contribute a clarifying identity to an entire quarter of a town. And it is this largest interval of scale that must be made to create visual order in the chaotic sprawl of our cities.

When the construction of Brasilia is nearer to completion, we will be able to observe the effect of a planned use of three modulations of the norm. They represent the functional divisions of the plan – a national centre, a city centre, and the residential superblocks – and they may suffice to contribute clarity to a city of its projected size. A huge modern city requires a more complex hierarchy of standards. The scale must be used to break the city down into intelligible units; and, in addition, it must be employed to reinforce the distinctions among them.

The Baroque treatment of scale according to a single standard of size, and our need to plan variations in the standard, parallels the difference between Baroque and Modern conceptions of architectural space. The Baroque world of space was, of course, intended to be seen by actual persons; and many of the architectural effects are designed to exploit the time sequences of perception. But the views of a moving observer were intended to be organized about fixed positions. And the controlling order of the space arrangements, shown in plans and sections, may be grasped in a single view. This is also true of Baroque scale. The controlling system for an entire environment – surrounded by its cushion of countryside – may be visualized at once as a concrete model, because the regulating order of scale is composed of variations on a single standard of largeness-smallness.

Only a small portion of a design that is organized as a continuum of space may be visualized in this simple manner. The views of the observer may be organized about evolving nuclei that shift as he moves. The larger order of the design, and the whole continuum of space defined, may be comprehensible only from a series of different positions seen at different times. Thus, there is a very important difference between Baroque and contemporary models for either space or scale. And although there is no practical difficulty in planning a peculiarly modern environment of scale (areas may be assigned on drawings, shapes may be arranged to establish different standards of size, and a spectator may be expected to observe them), we must anticipate that the regulating order will be impossible to visualize as a single scheme grasped at once. Each norm of largeness-smallness requires a different kind of inspection.

I do not wish to exaggerate these differences. An observer standing within an effective design, whether it is typically Baroque or uniquely contemporary, perceives what the designer intends him to see, without conscious rationalization. Plans and diagrams for contemporary buildings may be accurately interpreted merely by imagining one's self within the spaces defined. The differences are important here primarily because we are considering relationships of very large sizes. For this scope of designing, or of imagination, the regulating order of scale may not be visualized merely as a fixed arrangement. It must be understood as a scheme of variable relationships – combining variable standards of size with variable treatments of scale.

It is clear that we must discover a model for scale based upon variable relationships. The Baroque model shows that radical revisions are needed if it is to be accommodated to the practical problems of urban design in our time. But to an even greater extent, the Baroque system illustrates the uselessness of the older ways of imagining the visual relationships of very large sizes. For designs that are extensive in scope, and require modulations in the norm of size, its simplicity actually stands in the way of an understanding of the variable relationships that we expect. For designing of this scope, it cannot usefully be revised or extended. It must be discarded.

The New Model

We have been dealing with barren as well as fruitful ideas about the new environment of scale; and our comments have been extended to cover specific problems of designing. Abstracted from this context there are very few requirements.

The new model should be applicable to the entire environment. This is a practical trait because of the expanding scope of architecture and urban planning. And, in designing, it allows the modern architect's treatment of scale to parallel his treatment of defined space.

The new environment of scale should be based upon people's actual modes of perception in order to reflect accurately the relationship between architecture and human beings that we find emotionally satisfying. This provides an 'observer centred' orientation of scale which corresponds to the central consideration that the architect gives to the observer when he is designing a continuum of defined space.

The new model should allow architects to choose from the entire range of treatments of scale – small scale, normal scale, large scale, and variations in scale. This liberty is needed to solve the problems that accompany the new physical scale of our cities, and to ensure a treatment of scale that is charged with meaning. People's complicated preconceptions about sizes and relationships of sizes are an essential part of their cultural inheritance. Some of the lively intricacy of human activities and institutions should be communicated through architectural scale.

Finally, a new model for the environment of scale should allow the architect and the planner to design variations in the standard of largeness-smallness. This additional modulation of size is needed now to make the vast expanses of our cities intelligible. And it is implicit in the first characteristic described here: that the new model be capable of infinite extension.

These desirable traits may be very briefly summarized. The new world of scale must embrace the entire environment; it must be 'observer centred'; and it must allow a full range of treatments including the modulation of largeness-smallness itself. But it is clear that brevity is the only simple virtue of this list. Each specification stands for an important influence upon the treatment of scale; and as each trait is partially descriptive of a single model for an environment of scale, it must be assumed that each of them is part of a single concordant conception.

The search for a new model may conveniently be conducted in two stages. The first is the discovery of a way to imagine the traits that are required, in the relationships that are desired. A mere list of facts about the treatment of scale would be of little use to a designer. A useful model, like the Baroque system, provides a clearly imagined framework that the designer may work within. In our case, the framework must be one of double variable relationships; and by its nature we may expect that it will elude simple visualization as a picture. The other stage follows. Once we have found a way to imagine the nature of the regulating system that we need, we may define a useful model for an environment of scale.

The distinction between an analytical diagram and a design is familiar to architects. In designing a building that will house complicated movements of people, goods, or vehicles, it is usually convenient first to discover the abstract solution. This solution, expressed in a circulation diagram that shows the interweaving and connecting of movements, often suggests the generic arrangement of the building's design. Thus, the circulation diagram is not a design, but it may be an abstraction that solves the puzzle of desirable relationships. Other abstractions, with a similar relationship to the design, may be useful for buildings that must evoke a powerful emotional response. Le Corbusier refers to the shell of a crab as the first conception of the Ronchamp Chapel.[47] The crabshell, in this case, is no more the beginning of a building design than was the circulation diagram. But its evocative structural shape helped him to invent the building's original conception.

I expect that any of our specifications for a new world of scale, studied at length, would yield a useful diagram of this kind. Indeed, an entirely satisfactory solution to any of the problems

[47] Le Corbusier (C. E. Jeanneret-Gris), *Le Livre de Ronchamp*, Paris, 1916.

that are raised, for example the urban traffic problem, would contribute to a contemporary treatment for visual scale. But the central difficulty is a problem of imagination. The most direct assault upon it is an attempt to imagine a synthesis of the relationships that we have anticipated separately – to look for a vividly imagined abstract model that meets the requirements.

This brash approach promises an advantage over the more cautious ones. An entirely abstract preliminary model may be purely spatial. It may be related to, and even employ, the contemporary conception of spatial relationships. And of all our specifications for an environment of scale we found that the one that is the most consistently suggestive of a new model for designing is the requirement that it be compatible with the definition of a continuum of space.

Let us examine an easily imagined conception – like the circulation diagram or the crabshell – that will represent our requirements for a world of scale. There is a vivid image that represents a consolidation of our specifications; and it is commonly known and understood. Most small boys have, at some time, played at arranging and re-arranging a scattering of iron filings with a magnet. And those of us who have not actually experimented with a magnet and filings have seen them in pictures illustrating the forces of a magnetic field. Let us imagine a sheet of white paper on which dark iron filings have been scattered. The filings, following the pull of the magnetic poles, have been attracted to a typical pattern of curves and whorls. If the white of the paper is taken to represent largeness of scale and if the dark of the filings is taken for smallness of scale, a complete gradation may be seen, from light to dark, representing every variation of scale.

The variations are spread on the sheet so that transitions from light to dark, and from large scale to small scale, may be more or less abrupt or may be so graduated as to be almost imperceptible. But the changes of value are always the edges of larger shapes that they depend upon; and the large pattern of whorls and arcs– which may be taken to represent standards of largeness-smallness – is always coherent. There are small tight whorls and there are great sweeping arcs; but each shape is organically related to the other whorls and arcs in the over-all pattern of convolutions. As the magnetic field changes in intensity, or as the poles are given new positions, the patterns will be changed. But each change, and each new pattern, will provide the relationship of gradation to

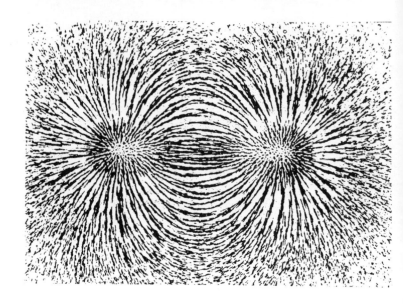

A complete gradation, representing every variation of scale

shape and the harmony of whorls which characterized the preceding patterns.

Because of the electrical currents, what might have been a uniform sprinkling of filings acquires the distinctive properties of an endless variation in response to changing forces and a maintenance of the two kinds of continuity – graduated change from light to dark, and organic relationship of whorls to each other. The analogy presented by this kind of a pattern cannot be read like a map from one point of view. But, read as a chart of forces, the relationships that it establishes are analogous to those which provide a free observer with a continuity of experience throughout the day – the natural 'unit' of scale. Wherever he goes, the observer may find a continuity of large-small scale experience and a continuity in standard of size. The response of the field to magnetic forces is analogous to the response of experience of scale to other forms of meaning – visual and nonvisual. And the shifting of the pattern, as the magnetic field changes, is analogous to the alterations in the perception of sizes which, with the passage of time, must accompany changes in context and meaning.

This flight of imagination, obviously, is no more certain than are other analogies. But it illustrates the way in which a set of relationships may be consistent and continuous – as superior visual experience must be – and may, nevertheless, provide for variations that are deliberately created by the architects, or reflect the observer's preconceptions, or march with changing times. Beyond this, the image of the magnetic field suggests another analogy that has a relationship to architectural scale which is much more than a mere analogy. It is taken from the remarkable maps and diagrams of Patrick Geddes,[48] one of the founders of modern urban planning; and we should examine it at some length.

In order to illustrate the investigation that should precede town planning, Geddes prepared studies of a typical European Valley Region. It was a geographical entity, defined on three sides by mountains and hills, on the fourth by the sea, and containing its own river, forests and fields. With this region as a unit, he was able to show the way in which some communities were founded to take advantage of geographical positions – a fishing village on the natural harbour, a ford city at the river's highest point of navigation, etc. And he was able to show the way in which other cities grew from the transportation links between the original communities, for example, a country town at the juncture of footpaths in a large arable district.

In one 'Valley Section', Geddes was able to illustrate the activities that naturally derive from the geography – quarrying and gold mining in the mountains, sheep farming on the heights, cattle farming on the plains below, market gardening in the fertile lands near the cities, and so on. In another 'Valley Section' he shows the more advanced activities that indirectly exploit the geography. These include iron and steel mills, goldsmiths, bakers, brewers, butchers, and the commercial port. In this way, Geddes invited attention to the order of growth in a region – its bases in the geography, and the natural development of complicated industrial and social activities from these beginnings. By showing their evolution in time, and by inviting attention to the interaction of physical and social forces, he sought to uncover the origins and the residual meanings of the modern town and its related countryside. Tracing the history of our institutions in this way, he sought to emphasize planning as the accommodation of a continual process of change. The evolution of institutions of all kinds, which took place in the relatively empty spaces of the region's early history, must continue. And now that the institu-

[48] Patrick Geddes, *Cities in Evolution*, New York, 1950.

Within the illustration the following labels appear:

HIGHEST
POI

COUNTRY TOWN
JUNCTION OF ROADS
AT FOOT OF PASS

PASS

C(

LOWEST BRIDGEABL
WORKS & FAC

BRIDGE &
FISHING VILLAGE

SEASIDE
RESORT

European valley region,

tions have become complicated and inter-related, the population has greatly increased and the open spaces are becoming filled up, it must be continued with the help of skilful planning. In other diagrams, Geddes attempted to create 'thinking machines' of folded paper, designed to show the interlocking of factors which connect human abilities to think and to feel with human activities and with the urban environment.

Geddes' Valley Region unit has been developed by his successors into the modern urban and regional planning disciplines that employ detailed studies and exact techniques for reducing the complicated patterns of relationship to manageable order. And to treat respectably today with the inter-relations suggested by

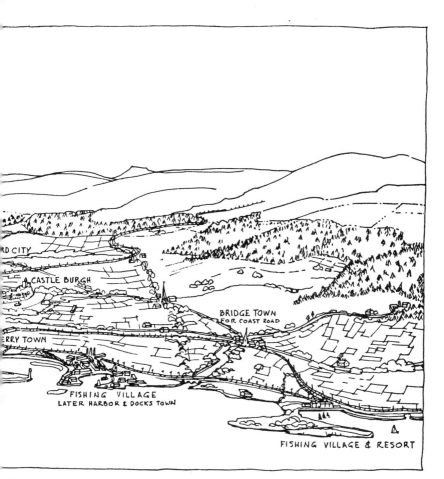

after Patrick Geddes' water-colour map

his paper thinking machines would require a board of demographers, sociologists, political scientists, economists, and even philosophers – each equipped with the skills and insights of his discipline. But Geddes' studies come close to describing the 'magnetic field' that, in the preceding analogy, warped and shaped the uniform grey norm of scale.

The observer's preconceptions and expectations of size (which, we discovered, affect his perception of sizes) are determined partly by the long history of the geography, its use and exploitation, and by the long evolution of economic and social institutions. And they are determined partly by the environment that these developments have provided him during his formative years – most directly, by the architectural environment in which he has lived. The observer's associations of scale with nonvisual meanings also affect his perceptions of size; and they are similarly determined by the history, by the culture and by the place itself. At another level, the broad standard of largeness-smallness, which he accepts as normal, can only be explained in the same way.

An environment studied in depth, as Geddes studied his Valley Region, is more than analogous to the continuum of scale. It comes close to representing exactly the forces that determine it, and that continually remodel it. Consequently, we are able to recognize in the Geddes Region, developed as a geographical historical unit, a larger entity into which townscaping studies – made with an all-embracing eye – are naturally linked. We may observe that it is the kind of a larger unit into which our microcosm of the spatial continuum may be easily fitted. And we may also observe that it is a larger unit that incorporates the levels of meaning which, in our study of human scale, we found an inherent part of the observer's own contributions to the perception of sizes.

I am suggesting that the new model for an environment of scale is essentially the architect's designing, in 'observer centered' variable human scale, within the context of the environment as it is found, and as it may be most thoroughly understood. The best way to show that it is a working model – that it provides a designer with a useful understanding of the relationships of scale – is to show how it is used. This is the principal method of illustration that I shall employ. In doing so, I shall be able to show that it is not an entirely new conception but the product of a long tradition that has left its mark on architecture and urban design. But the illustrations may be clearer if we are prepared for some of the surprising traits of the system. It will be obvious, for instance, that it is not only a new model but also a different kind of model; and because of this it may seem an elusive one.

For all of the subtlety and elegance of Baroque buildings and squares, the Baroque model for scale could be paraphrased as a formula – there were relationships that the architect sought and relationships that he did not seek. Because of this, it was possible on a single page to describe a typical town's arrangement of streets, squares, ordinary buildings, and public monuments. This arrangement may be imagined as a mythical city. And when each of the executed works of Baroque architecture is imagined as placed within it, a position and a relationship of scale may be found for it without much adjustment either of the city or of the building. Nothing of the sort is possible with the new model. It does not specify the final results of a treatment of scale, but rather sets a way of establishing it. And as the way of establishing a treatment of scale takes into account the observer's subjective responses and the context of the design as it is found, we cannot imagine a typical conformation. There is none.

Indeed, we may observe that the chief trait of the new model is, somewhat paradoxically, a rejection of the idea of a concrete model. In the place of a system that establishes a norm of largeness-smallness and specifies typical relationships of scale – between buildings, and between buildings and open spaces – the new model substitutes a way for the designer to control them. For each condition of the architectural context it prescribes the treatment of scale that is appropriate: a designed solution.

The context that influences architectural scale includes all of the factors – past and present, local or regional – which are represented in Geddes's Valley Region. The Geddes Region may be considered as a schematic representation of the complete study that should underlie serious urban or regional planning. His illustrations – easily grasped and understood at once – represent the shelves of study documents, rolls of drawings, and the extensive bibliography that is needed for a thorough planning study; and this material can be neither quickly grasped nor easily understood. To be comprehended, a modern proposal for a city plan may require weeks, or even months, of careful examination. And it is not likely that any individual will be sufficiently erudite to appreciate every detail of it. It correlates studies in many special fields, such as land economy, traffic control, tax structure, and population distribution; and each field has its special discipline. Nevertheless, it is this complicated area of study that I am suggesting as one of the bases for a useful understanding of the relationships of scale. But in doing so I shall be able to show that for an architect, or for an urban planner, the control of scale need not be a nightmare of abstraction and complexity.

We may observe at the onset that the diagrammatic nature of planners' charts, social scientists' reports or zoning ordinances, differs fundamentally from the diagrammatic nature of the infinitely extended modules of physical scale or of over-simple human scale to which I have vehemently objected. We have repeatedly questioned the value of visual criteria that may elude perception or tend to escape a designer's most vivid imaginings. We were, for example, suspicious of the precisions of proportional systems where they might not be perceived, or where they might be perceived differently in different contexts. But when we apply the same scrutiny to the documents of urban planning, there is an important difference. Much of the architectural context that they establish may be directly perceived by an architect standing in the street and looking about him, and need not be questioned. Other parts of it, such as zoning ordinances or building laws, are initially far removed from direct visual experience. But as ordinances or regulations are carried out, and as they become realized in tangible buildings, streets and squares, their printed prescriptions emerge as concretely defined as are room shapes or building masses. Similarly, the abstractions of a traffic control pattern may first appear as a diagram on paper, but as it is constructed to form roads, bridges and traffic interchanges, these take their place in the visible world as concretely as building shapes, hills or trees. Thus, although their visual qualities are at first latent, a designer may anticipate them as vividly as he imagines the other portions of his designs; and later they may be experienced as directly by an observer. It is not the abstract quality of these determinants that sets them off from other visual qualities, but their size. The entirety of the masses, spaces and sizes that they control may be so large that it may be experienced by an observer only over a considerable period of time.

Realization of this sort is not possible with the abstractions of a human-sized module, infinitely extended, or of physical scale divisions, automatically exhibited. These may also be incorporated into designs and seen; but the restriction of the measuring system to inflexible units that can neither reflect the meaning inherent in buildings nor offer the varied experience of scale that makes very large designs intelligible, renders them ineffective. By their nature they paralyse our ability to apprehend them.

Finally, before examining the new world of scale in operation we may inquire if it is infinitely extendible. This requirement headed our list of specifications; yet the examples of an architectural context that we have considered – the Geddes Valley Region, and modern regional or urban plans – are attached to circumscribed areas. They are, of course, bounded in this way merely because they have not been extended comprehensively. The scope of this form of study may be extended to embrace any area. But we may observe that they are not likely to be extended uniformly.

Even if we could match the scope of planning to the need for planning, it would not impartially extend to the whole world. No doubt some world-wide functions would call for global planning, for example airport facilities or, perhaps, defence establishments. Others such as railroads, forest preserves, or hydro-electric systems would be given a national or regional scope. But it seems clear that the bulk of planning would be where it is at present – following the concentrations of population and buildings in urban and suburban areas. In short, the scope of the continuum of scale may correspond everywhere to the need for planning. And because of this the system may be considered infinitely extendible for our purposes. But in actuality, it would be carried out in a series of overlapping areas in which the degree of control matches the need for it.

This form of extension closely parallels the architect's treatment of a continuum of defined space which is also theoretically infinite in extent. Practically, an architect defines the portion of the space that he is concerned with, accommodates other portions by adjusting his designs to them, and inevitably leaves most of the continuous world of space undesigned. Correspondingly, we may observe that although the area of study typified by an urban planner's work establishes the bases for an environment of scale – and that it certainly must concern architects – it is no more an albatross around his neck than the continuum of space is a requirement that he study the physics of space-time. To design within a theoretically infinite space and scale continuum, the architect needs what he has always needed: a grasp of the connection between the area under his control and the larger area that surrounds it, and may be relevant to design decisions. And if the essentially extra-visual model of the planner is accepted as a proper basis for an understanding of a continuum of scale, it can be shown that he is amply supplied with these visual connections.

Today, skilful analyses of the architectural landscape are almost exclusively English in origin or inspiration. The reason for this is the attitude toward the visible environment that was first developed in the English water-colour school of landscape painters – from Cozens through Constable.[49] It has continued to shape the outlook of some of the Englishmen interested in architecture; and in our time it affords a preparation for the distinctively

[49] *English Watercolours*, introduced by Lawrence Binyon, New York, 2nd ed. 1962.

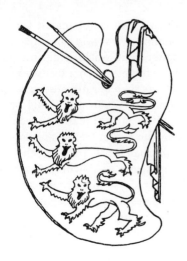

Almost exclusively English

modern approach to planning that is rivalled only, if at all, by the older landscape painting tradition of the Netherlands.

The water-colour school originated as 'topographic' painting – distinguished by a sheer love of nature and a factual, if not literal, description of the landscape. And as the mature water-colour school developed an attitude toward the landscape that was romantically sensitive to movement and scene, it retained to a remarkable degree the habit of factual description. Even in the most casual-appearing sketches, the painter's eye seems not only to have sought out the evocative and pleasing patterns of a scene, but also to have searched out its lineaments, as if actually exploring the limits of the landscape depicted. Typically, everything before the eyes is treated in much the same way – as related in the view; and John Constable's statement, 'I have never looked at any object unconnected with a background or other objects',[50] is entirely believable. In the paintings and drawings of Cotman, in particular, this impartial outlook is extended to architecture, which – whether it is humble or grand – is treated as yet another element in the landscape. Thus, the painters established a tradition for the perception of a view which is essentially the 'all-embracing eye' that we recognized as inherent in the spatial approach to architectural designing.

Aside from its influence on the main line of British and Continental painters, the visual tradition established the outlook of

[50] Ibid. John Constable quoted by Binyon.

Rough and often merely quaint

many amateurs of painting, and exerted a powerful influence even where the observer's interests were not primarily aesthetic. Patrick Geddes, whose Valley Region supplied our example of the environment affecting scale, is an interesting case in point. Because of the habit of looking at his surroundings in the landscape manner, Geddes managed to outline a procedure for studying the visual alterations to Pittencrieff Park, Dunfermline, which is unexceptionable.[51] He sought out the views of the place with an eye for the picturesque and a cool assessment of the facts of the scene. He divided the estate into areas that were visual and practical entities; and he made an extensive photographic survey that not only depicted each area in detail but also recorded the seasonal changes of summer, autumn, winter and spring. Alterations to the Park were presented for consideration only after they had been sketched, in place, on the photographic negatives, and tried out on a contour model of the entire park. Geddes' specific proposals are rough, and often merely quaint; and it is clear that his principal interests are sociological rather than visual. But his easy mingling of practical and visual facts, and his bold leap to study the landscape from within, derive from the landscape painter's view of the environment.

The outlook of the English water-colourists is still alive. As might be expected, its influence may be traced in academic painting where it accounts for much of what is refreshing. But it has also survived, and has been revitalized, in the paintings of the

---

[51] Patrick Geddes, *City Development, a Study of Parks, Gardens and Cultural Institutions*, Birmingham, 1904.

modern school; and it characterizes much of the modern work, figurative or abstract, which may be said to be distinctively English. The connections between the traditional landscape way of looking at the environment and the revolutionary conceptions of modern art are perhaps most obvious to architects. But they have been lucidly described in the paintings and the illustrated essays of John Piper.[52] And when he writes about the architectural landscape – as he does in his essay on 'The Nautical Style' – he provides a modern extension through photographs and drawings of Cotman's explorations of the landscape as it is found. And he speaks in a language that appeals directly to the architectural designer at his work.

It is the outlook that never perceives objects unrelated to each other and to the scene which makes the landscape tradition especially valuable in the visual planning of architecture and of cities. The effects of architecture and urban design are observed with a painter's subtle awareness of nuance and movement. There is an intimate appreciation of the relationships between the function and the site of a building and its visual character – as they are found in the view – so that it is accepted as a reasonable and obvious connection. At the same time, the all-embracing eye provides a solution to problems of historical styles and 'what is architecture' which were for a long time bothersome to architects. Old or new, 'bicycle shed' or 'cathedral', buildings are treated as objects related to each other and to the landscape in the view. In short, everything that is before the eyes is drawn into a single network of visual relationships, which the reader will recognize as the relationships that the observer, in fact, perceives. Thus, while the English landscape painting tradition has nothing to do with the definition of a continuum of space (although the landscaping of some English parks comes close to doing just this), the way of looking at a view closely resembles that of the spatially oriented architect.

With this inheritance, a group of English architects and planners have demonstrated that the visual planning of towns of moderate size is possible; and in the process, they have illustrated the new model for architectural scale. The way to begin is, of course, to investigate. Because of the close connection between the visual and the practical – and between physical scale and visual scale – the investigation for visual design cannot be con-

[52] John Piper, *Buildings and Prospects*, London, 1948.

210

fined to what impresses the eye. Consequently, the techniques of urban research, which have been developed under the tutelage of the social sciences, are needed for visual as well as practical planning. Many of them may profitably be applied as routines for surveying the site and the activities that take place in it. The visual investigation of the site, by contrast, is much more intimate and personal. Very little of it can be reduced to a formula, as the visual data that is needed is the very opposite of the routine – the facts that determine the distinctive visual character of places.

The initial decisions of visual planning are, in a sense, the most important ones. They must determine, practically and visually, what distinguishes a particular town from the others, and establish the distinctive places within it. In order to make these decisions wisely, the place must be studied in depth – in the Geddes manner – investigating what it was, what it is, and what it may become.

What a place has been largely determines the observer's preconceptions about it. Consequently, historical research is not only useful to determine the value of the monuments that have survived from the past; it also helps the designer to anticipate the way that new designs, in the same place, will be perceived. The context of the past is both visible, having left its mark upon the site, and invisible, as it conditions the observer's own contributions to perception.

What a place is, obviously, is the very material to be assessed; and it must be scrutinized with the persistence and curiosity of a news reporter. In this task the all-embracing eye is especially valuable, as it protects the designer from the blind spots which might lead him to overlook or to ignore some of the visual facts of the place. With the landscape outlook he will not see a mansion but fail to see a shack, for instance; and he will not automatically appreciate the character of a Georgian church and condemn, without seeing them, the qualities of a Ruskinian meeting hall.

The question of what is to be done requires the designer's keenest skill in observing potentialities of a place, and calls for his shrewdest planning to discern what may be achieved economically. Here, the landscape tradition is valuable because it studies the problem within the context of the place. The future development of the site is apt to be woven into the existing place; and the urban designer is not likely to bring to the site a shoe box, representing the volume of a building, and search for an opening to set it in (as one renowned American architect has done). Even if he decides that the place must be swept clean and designed anew, the decision and the new design will be made for the place.

The investigations and the decisions of the visual planner are not made merely to secure a list of places and their conspicuous features, or to compile a roster of the monuments to be preserved. It is his particular skill to observe and to develop a sound judgment as to exactly what distinguishes, and did characterize, and should properly differentiate one place from another. In some instances his final evaluation may be ravishingly simple. Gordon Cullen was able to study four seaside towns, and for each of them to find in the way that the town should meet the sea a simple and direct controlling order for the visual design.[53] Thus, in his scheme for Lyme Regis as in the three other schemes, it is the line where the land meets the sea that frames his major recommendations. And it is from the existing character of the town – also derived from the seaside location – that he develops his more detailed recommendations.

The distinctive characteristics that Cullen discovers at Lyme Regis, and his recommendations for its visual planning, provide ample material for the control of variable human scale as we understand it. A standard of largeness-smallness is set by the waterfront itself. It begins at the Cobb, a harbour made of curving stone jetties, extends along the arc of the Marine Parade to the Square, which has a stone ramp extending into the water on the side that is open to the sea. Beyond the Square there is an opening in the sea wall for the mouth of the river and then the Gun Cliff rises on a rock, with walls that fall straight into the sea.

Cullen suggests that the sea wall of the Marine Parade, and the terraces of houses that line it, should be extended to the Cobb. With this link in place, the water front is joined into a continuous walkway, is expressed in a single lucid formal gesture, and is given a single visual scale that 'measures' all of the incidents of the sea front – from fishing boats to taverns. The scale of the Cobb and the completed sea wall is considerably larger than the usual village residential scale. But it is easy to over-estimate it, because the walls – joined into a continuous line of the simple shapes and flowing curves that efficiently hold the sea in check – develop an emotional response of 'feeling of bigness' that is unusual at this scale. As the combination of large (but not extremely large) scale

[53] Gordon Cullen, 'The Line of Life', *Architectural Review*, Aug. 1950 and 'The Functional Tradition', Jan. 1950. See also *Townscape*, London and New York, 1961.

and impressive feeling of bigness distinguishes the entire sweep
of the water front, it carries a standard of scale to the entire length
of the town. On the one hand, as long as the place remains a fishing and resort town, no larger scale may be used, for it would
senselessly compete in importance with the jetties and sea walls.
On the other hand, the simple grandeur of the stone sea walls may
be counted on to show up and to condemn any serious lapses into
triviality or fussiness in the design of the buildings that are seen
with it. Thus, a model is found for the treatment of scale in the
most important part of the town; and it is based on the practical
and visual facts of the place.

The nature of the place also indicates treatments of scale in
some detail. It is clear, for example, that the scale of the houses to
be built along the extended Marine Parade calls for some skill in
designing. Each house, considered by itself, should be in a modest
small scale commensurate with its function as a private residence,
inn, or holiday rooming house. But the house is a unit of the whole
crescent shaped wall of houses that follows the curve of the sea
wall. This calls for a larger scale. For, although the scale of these
houses may be much smaller than the scale of the sea wall that
protects them, it must be large enough to face the open space of
the sea. For the same reason, the entire sweep of buildings should
have shapes and colours that are neat and clear when they are
seen from a considerable distance. And breaks in the continuity
of the formal arrangement – for example, a wide variety in the
shapes and heights of roofs – would create spots of fragile fuss in
the long line of houses, and should be avoided.

The treatment of scale in other parts of the town is less exacting, but no less implicit in the facts of the place. The Square presents a framework for scale that is similar to that of the houses of
the Marine Parade. But the buildings that are set back from the
water may be scaled to the enclosed space in the Square and to
their function as houses and shops. The brunt of the problem of
openness falls on the buildings that flank the opening to the sea.
In the narrow inside streets, sheltered from the sea, the scale may
be residential; the feeling of bigness may be relaxed; and some
fussiness may be welcomed. The carrying powers of the shapes
and colours may be variously set by the width of the narrow
streets, or by the short vistas that are opened down their length.

It may be a little confusing to discover that Cullen's seaside
town, which I have used to illustrate the new model for scale, was
originally published under the title 'The Functional Tradition'.

I have discussed the scale treatment of Lyme Regis because it is a relatively simple example of the modern approach to visual planning. It was entitled 'The Functional Tradition'[54] because most of its structures show a commonsense relationship between function, construction and visual design. But the coincidence of the new model for visual planning and the functional tradition in designing is altogether appropriate. A commonsense relationship between functional and visual designs greatly simplifies the modern approach to the visual planning of towns. The relationship between use, construction, materials and appearance, is close to the heart of any philosophy of designing. And although we may hope that it will some day be given enough study to protect it from the willi-waws of architectural fashion, it seems likely that it will always be susceptible to various emphases and interpretations. But satisfactory interpretations are apt to be close to the functional tradition in designing. It ensures that the function of a building or of a street shall be closely related to its appearance, and that the design for physical scale and for visual scale shall be harmoniously co-ordinated. This is a wholesome influence: it brings together in designing the practical and visual factors that the observer understands and perceives together.

A visual planner's assessment of distinctive character must be based on the facts of the place. And even when an analysis is as penetrating and as clear as Gordon Cullen's, it may not often be understandable as a single visual-functional conception. Thomas Sharp's recommendations for the post-war rebuilding of Exeter show the complexity that ordinarily arises from the facts of a town of modest size.[55] The Cathedral and its Close are undoubtedly the most important monuments of the town. But in Exeter – as opposed to Chartres, for example – the cathedral is not an overwhelmingly large building, nor do its activities dominate the present-day life of the town. The largest distinctive unit of Exeter is the portion of the town within the old city walls. And to make this unit clear Sharp proposed that the wall be preserved in a new green belt. But within this walled city there are several distinctive quarters in addition to the Cathedral and Close. The street that comprises the main shopping district bisects the old town. There

[54] Gordon Cullen, *Architectural Review*, Jan. 1950.

[55] Thomas Sharp, *Exeter Phoenix*, London, 1946. See also *English Panorama*, London, 1938, *Newer Sarum*, London, 1949, *Oxford Replanned*, London, 1948, *Town Planning*, Harmondsworth, Middlesex, 1940, *The Anatomy of the Village*, Harmondsworth, 1946.

were large bombed-out areas that presented the opportunity for the practical and visual revitalization of the town. The height of Exeter Castle is occupied by the Assize Hall, and is flanked by a college. There are prosperous residential areas with rows of fine old houses, and there are depressed ones that have never been well built. Each quarter within the wall has its character and its problems.

Outside the old town, there are other entities, practical or visual. Some are residential districts, some are manufacturing areas; and they spread to the surrounding hills, to the river, or stop at valuable rural areas that resist encroachment. Thus, while Exeter may be characterized as a cathedral town, a tourist attraction, a market centre, and a town that supplies services to the surrounding countryside, it cannot be summed up in a phrase or in a simple visual statement. Even after careful investigation, its character must be, by and large, its unique combination of the distinctive places of the town.

For each of the large quarters of Exeter, Sharp suggested somewhat different governing principles for visual design. The Close, for example, should preserve its urbane mixture of houses and shops, churches and inns; and it should be improved by additions that faithfully reflect its 'almost continental' vivacity. The bombed-out areas, by contrast, should be replanned in new, more useful, street patterns; and the new buildings should contribute a new visual character. In each instance, Sharp's suggestions for visual planning provide us with the criteria for the treatment of variable human scale. In any one of the town's quarters, the relationship of the unit to the neighbouring quarters of the town is a help. The scale treatment is not established in limbo, but is framed within the context of the surrounding places. And in each quarter there is a characteristic scale or a distinctive combination of scales. These may be provided by blocks of existing buildings, or by buildings planned for the site; by the scale appropriate to the street widths and open squares, existing or planned; by the scale of important individual buildings that may punctuate or consolidate the scale of the structures around them; and by the scale of the topography itself.

Thus, the architect planning a building is not in the position of originating a scale for it. He knows from the beginning of his design that his structure must be in a scale determined by what the building is and where it is. And because the urban planner looked for places of distinctive character – rather than trying to soak the town in the gravy of a uniform visual character and scale – this appropriate scale may be larger or smaller than the scale of the neighbouring buildings. Indeed, it is where the functional meaning and the architectural context of a building are most seriously considered that we may expect contrasts in scale – between a bank and a bakery shop, or between the cathedral and the neighbouring housing. In a town with a long history and a great variety of activities, the wealth of meaning inherent in the place calls for vivacity in the treatment of scale.

In most towns that are the size of Exeter, these variations in scale may be conveniently considered as departures from a single standard of largeness-smallness. In Sharp's Exeter, the norm is framed between the moderately large scale of the Cathedral and of the new arterial roads and the smaller scale of the residential blocks. But this is only a convenient way to think of the variations in scale, and a recognition of the fact that the main features of the town are quickly grasped. Where there is a reason to divide a town into two places, it may be convenient to consider that there are two standards of size. At Laon in France, for example, where there is an old cathedral town on a hill and a new town growing below, two standards of largeness-smallness might heighten the inevitable contrasts between the two parts of the town. At Exeter, and in the typical town of its size, new projects are constructed among the old buildings; and a similar change of norms would be disruptive and meaningless.

It should be clear by now that the distinction between a norm of scale and largeness or smallness of scale, which was necessary to explore the Baroque model, is a matter of convenience for us. The difference is one of time. It is convenient to use the terms norm of scale, or standard of largeness-smallness, where a large-small scale treatment is sustained long enough to establish in the observer a definite expectation of size that serves as his base assumption of largeness-smallness. As a rule, the distinctive quarters of a town are not experienced long enough, and are not sufficiently isolated, to provide the observer with this conditioning.

It is when we consider the treatment of scale in a very large city that the convenient distinction between a standard of size and largeness or smallness of scale becomes very useful. There is no reason why a large city cannot be visually planned in much the same way as a modest town, using additional levels of observation and planning for the very large distinctive areas. The whole city may be broken down into great sections that are comparable in size to the town of Exeter, or much larger, as the visual and functional factors of the place may indicate. Obviously, the larger the city is the more clean distinctions must be used, and the more clearly they must be made. But we should observe the effect of the size and scale of the whole city upon our understanding of its parts. We may expect for a large city that there shall not only be more distinctive places, but that they shall be larger than they would be in a small town. Correspondingly, we expect that the few distinctive places in a small town shall be smaller. Thus, a city that is quite small, but is able to support many of the activities of a larger one, may have a complexity of activities that is expressed in an almost toy-like virtuosity of visual design and in an unusual vivacity of scale treatment.

We may not, then, think of a metropolis as made up of great sections that are 'towns' of buildings with practical and visual affinities. The 'magnetic field' which warps the fabric of human scale tends to enlarge only slightly the scale of the small places within the city. A private courtyard in a city, or an ordinary street, for example, will tend to be merely somewhat larger than its small-town counterpart. But there is an accelerated enlargement of the larger parts. The large streets and squares of a modern metropolis tend to be very much larger in size than their small-town counterparts. The great distinctive sections that are peculiar to very large cities must be thought of as very large indeed. Their distinctive visual character and scale will normally be experienced for considerable periods of time, while the observer is surrounded by the section and it dominates his impressions. Because of this, he is likely to acquire definite expectations of size that become his base assumption of largeness-smallness.

We have referred to the disruptive effect of a similar change of norms when an observer drives through the successive 'growth rings' of our unplanned cities in rapid succession. In the compact sections of a great city, the norm of scale may be firmly established; and when the norm for one great section contrasts with that of another, the transition may be clearly marked and prepared, or softened by a transitional sequence of scales. Within these sections, the quarters may have their own variations of the standard – or in some cases be islands of contrasting scale, large enough to be distinguished, but not experienced long enough to monopolize all views or to be firmly established as a norm of size.

There is no doubt that within a town, large or small, ample visual and practical reasons are present to indicate the range of scales that a designer should work within. The peculiar anarchistic, visually chaotic, treatments of scale that are often found in our cities do not usually derive from difficult problems in the treatments of scale. They are the results of a failure to establish clearly the criteria outside the individual building which would enable the architect reasonably to prefer one treatment over another. These, essentially, hang upon an agreement as to what a place should be, as opposed to other places. When cities are being rapidly built up or – as is more often the case – when they are being rapidly torn down and then built up again piecemeal, there will always be some difficulty in establishing the character of a place. For it is obvious that the clearest indication of a particular character is to have it established in the architecture and the life of the place. But in lieu of this ideal, much may be accomplished through practical and visual planning toward distinctions, rather than toward a levelling by regulations.

When visual planning is carried out in the commonsense tradition, with the landscape concern for the facts of the place, the obligations and opportunities of the individual architect are in the classical balance that is essential to freedom. As in the spatial approach to designing, the principal obligation of the designer becomes the source of the greatest freedom. It is the comprehensive nature of the spatial approach to designing that permits the architect the widest freedom of choice: his designs may be dominated by planes, masses, or space-defining shapes and colours; they may be fragmented, self-contained, or parts of a flowing continuum of defined space. Similarly, the new model for scale imposes the responsibility for designing within a larger context of scale; but this obligation creates the greatest freedom as to how the architect shall weave his design into it. The test of his treatment of scale, then, is not whether he has designed in one scale or another, but whether he has joined his design with the scales that exist or that are planned for the place. Properly understood, the restrictions imposed by the context are invitations to create ingenious and varied treatments of scale. And for very large cities, we have seen that this opportunity is vital to coherence.

That the large structure of a city does exist in the observer's experience, as well as in the planner's diagrams and sketches, has been demonstrated in an interesting fashion by Kevin Lynch in *The Image of The City*.[56] Using the polling techniques of the

[56] Kevin Lynch, *The Image of the City*, Cambridge, Mass., 1960.

social scientists, Lynch was able to determine the large patterns of space arrangement that, for the man in the street, were memorable, and to distinguish those parts of a city that were 'grey areas', making little or no impression. Because the investigation stressed sequences of spatial impressions, the report may emphasize these qualities at the expense of others that are as important. But there is no reason to question what is, perhaps, the most interesting fact to emerge from the studies of Boston, Jersey City and Los Angeles: there is a close correspondence between the ordinary citizen's image of a city and the conceptions of it that would be anticipated by a spatially oriented designer.

Let us follow the expanding continuum of defined space – and of scale – and consider the region that lies outside the city. Any city, however large, is surrounded by natural or man-made landmarks which create a context of visual scale. But the context is not always perceived directly. We should distinguish between the scale of these large features of the landscape that may be seen from the city, or may be seen with the city – as the mountains and the bay are seen to encircle Rio de Janeiro – and the scale of features that are too vast to be seen and must be recalled from memory.

The often-cited – typically American – Centre City, located in a tan rectangular state of the Middle West, is a good illustration of the influence that is exerted by scales that are held in memory. It is supposed to lie in the centre of the Great Plains that stretch as far as the eye can see. With its rectangular grid of streets set in the larger rectangular grid of section roads, it is supposed to be as completely lacking, in the large topographical features that make a place distinctive, as a city can be. What is its context of scale?

When the inhabitants of Centre City emerge from their houses and venture into the open country, or when they catch sight of the great plain from within the city, they measure the landscape with two great markers that are not seen but, nevertheless, remain alive in the memory. To the west there is the snow covered pile of the Rocky Mountain Range, and that is where the plain finally ends. To the east, there is a great river; and the plain, gently tilting, sheds all of its water into it. These hidden features help to set the scale of the plain itself. It stretches to the horizon and places a large scale and large dimensions before the eyes; but it also carries a feeling of bigness and a largeness of scale that is derived from what is remembered, but not seen.

The rectangular sections that are bordered by the highways are also remembered rather than seen. But as they are frequently travelled, the memory of their size and shape is often renewed by new visual evidence. Certainly, Centre City is commonly thought of as sitting in the corner of the remembered rectangular section, and as tied to the remembered highway grid. Another important factor of scale which is remembered and may also be directly observed is the identification of a part of the plain as the area around Centre City. Parts of it are distinguished by their position next to the city, other parts are a good distance out, and some parts of it are so far out that their relationship to the city is hardly felt. Finally, this portion of the plain – which extends from the Rockies to the river, which is divided into section rectangles by the roads, and which is polarized around Centre City – is farming land. South of the city the crop is well above the ground, and the huge rectangular fields are swept with green waves. North of the city some of the plants in smaller fields are barely above the ground, and some of the fields lie fallow. The slightest differences in the drainage of the land, in the composition of the soil, or in the quality of husbandry, contribute a local quality, and a quality of scale, to the farmland.

This fictional city does not exist out of context. What is interesting, of course, is the vast openness of the level plain that it is on. How may a city, which is continually expanding around the perimeter, properly face the large-scale elements of the landscape? What an amazing conversation the city would have with the plain, if its outer edge could be made to face the openness with the boldness of the sea walls of Lyme Regis!

Centre City is the extreme case; but portions of the scale-giving context that must be held in memory are not unusual. Every schoolboy in Virginia, for example, knows that the state is a geological progression that begins where the sea invades the flat Tidewater plain, rises to the undulations of the Piedmont region, and ends in the Appalachian Mountain Range. The child probably cannot describe the visual scales that typify these formations, which are measured in hundreds of miles. But he holds the three great divisions in memory; and his experience of the character peculiar to each of them is not less real because he cannot explain it.

The Virginia mountains are a Switzerland worn down. And in them, as in the Alps, distances and heights are bound together. The mountains enclose the horizontal distances, but measure the

Switzerland worn down

The most versatile region

heights. In the valleys the views are relatively short, or up. From the heights the long distances unfold, and they may be unusually long. The shape of the earth itself gives each part of the map a visual frame and sets a visual scale for the place enclosed.

The rolling Piedmont hills are the most versatile region. By setting his University on a hill of no great size, Thomas Jefferson was able to create an academic village that, from within, could measure itself against the distance to the low mountains that ring the horizon, and see the fussy shapes of the intervening country reduced to a green floor of little consequence. But in the town nearby, a depression between hills may become for the residents

*Tidewater
plains are
solemn*

a world in itself. Filling the view in every direction, it may have
its own miniature slopes, its short vistas, and its own small scale.

The flat Tidewater plains are solemn. The horizon stays low,
and the sky is huge. The flat fields are large (but not as large as
those of the Middle West); and they are broken only by dark
windbreaks of pine trees. Where the water invades the land, great
spaces are opened in the landscape which is already empty. But
what is striking is the constancy of the measure of the land. There
are no dimpling hills or dramatic mountains to define new places
as we move. It is an invitation to classical order, to consistency in
a standard of size, or to great simple modulations of scale. In the
face of this landscape, the scale of buildings may be designed
small; but a fall from feeling of bigness into triviality is disastrous.

The great features of the visible world, that can be joined with
cities and buildings only in the memory, are the largest context of
scale. And where they are so large as to become the arena for a
person's entire life, like the great geological regions, they shape
many of the basic assumptions that colour his preconceptions of
size and of relationships of size.

The size of a region for visual planning, like the size of a town,
may vary greatly. The geographical and visual unit that makes the
most clearly defined region may be a river basin of continental
dimensions, or it may be a mountain gorge only a few miles
across. But the size need not be an indication of the amount of
visual planning that will be needed. Away from the concentrations of population, we may expect that there will be little inven-

tive planning, and that the treatment of visual scale will properly be confined to modestly accommodating new elements to the character that is already established. The planned visual elements may be confined to traffic arteries, to afforestation and the control of soil erosion, and to a few projects that need special attention in order to be fitted into the countryside. Most of what is seen may retain its character 'as found'. This will be particularly the case where, throughout a region, the distinctive visual character of the different *kinds* of land use are clearly recognized, maintained and heightened.

The failure to do this is a modern disease that has been labelled 'subtopia'. In England, in Europe, and conspicuously in the United States, the habit of regarding the open countryside as a worthless commodity to be recklessly filled with 'improvements' has been inherited from former times, when cities were still very small in the empty countryside, and when populations were sparse and scattered. As a consequence, each year vast stretches of the rural landscape are converted into commercial and residential developments that are neither town nor country; and the countryside is increasingly dotted with roadways, buildings and furnishings that are of uniform design – for no place. In the process, the functional and visual qualities that distinguish one place from another are rapidly disappearing into a common character that is utopian – in that it everywhere establishes an arbitrary 'ideal' – and of substandard quality because it substitutes mindless conformity for designing.

It is the editors of the *Architectural Review*,[57] again, who have led the discussion of this problem. They have suggested that a minimum of five distinctive categories of place should be recognized in Great Britain and strictly observed. The exact definitions that they have supplied are too lengthy to be reproduced here. But it is significant that each of them is not only a distinctive kind of visual character but also a category of treatment for scale. Wild regions and truly rural regions should be maintained in the character and the treatment of scale that they derive from nature, or from typically rural industries such as farming, forestry or cattle grazing. The suburbs of a town should be Arcadian; that is to say, they should maintain the 'ideally rustic' character that suburbs should have but increasingly do not. Consequently, Arcadia

[57] Special issues edited by Ian Nairn, 'Outrage', June 1955, 'Counter-Attack', Dec. 1956, *The Architectural Review*. Re-published as books with same titles, Architectural Press, London, 1955 and 1957.

should maintain a dainty scale treatment that is the very small scale of architecture – approaching the pixy, but never stepping across the line into caricature. A town should be distinctly different – compact, full of life, and enclosed – and its treatment of scale should reflect the complexity and the vitality of the place. A metropolis requires a large civic scale, with the variations appropriate to its size and complicated structure. The arterial highways should be considered as a separate category and maintain their own character and scale as they sweep across the countryside. Each region, like each city, has an over-all visual character and scale that distinguishes it from other regions. And within a region there is a treatment of scale appropriate to each kind of development, and vitally necessary to its character as a distinctive place.

The new model for an environment of scale provides that the treatment of scale for a city shall be designed within the scale of the surrounding region. This context is established, in part, by the scale of an environment that is too large to be seen, but is vividly remembered. And it is partly established by the large features of the landscape – mountains, valleys, highways, rivers, etc. – which are seen from the city and with it, and which determine the visual scale to which it is related in the view. The first step in designing the connection between the scale of the city and that of the surrounding region is an investigation in order to establish the distinctive character of the region. Around some cities there is an embarrassing wealth of visual interest and a confusion of scales; and the planner's initial effort may be to discover its essential simplifying order. Around other cities, a very few elements and a single statement of scale may acquire unusual importance because they alone dominate the scene. But there is normally sufficient material to determine the character of this larger nucleus of the continuum of defined space and scale.

To evaluate it, the planner needs the skill to discriminate among kinds of character. Upon a thorough understanding of what has – in the past – been the nature of the place, of its present visual and practical facts, and of its potentialities, he must determine what the visual character and its scale should become. His determination of the city's scale parallels that of the architect working within the city. The task does not impose a specific large, small, or normal scale upon the city's design; rather, his treatment of scale may be appreciated according to the skill with which it has been designed into the context of the region.

Where there is ordinary, practical, regional planning, the visual planner's work is greatly simplified. Regional planning normally includes practical studies of the region's topography, resources, population and institutions. The plan usually makes recommendations for the future development of some elements, such as the road system or the water-power resources; and it may allocate areas within the region for special uses, as in an industrial park or in a wild life preserve. But we may expect that in a region that is already well developed the planner's recommendations will affect only a small portion of the region's area. It is in the areas around the big cities, or in the portions of the region where populations are rapidly increasing and land uses rapidly changing, that the planner is apt to recommend a measure of control over an entire area.

If the urban planner's visual observations are acute, or if he has access to expert advice, this kind of a practical survey and plan makes a tolerable basis for designing the city's scale into the context of the region. There is likely to be enough correspondence between a practical arrangement and its appearance, and between the controls needed for practical and for visual planning, for him to anticipate correctly the visual scale of the region, as it exists and as it will be developed. Ideally, visual planning should go much further, to present a clear visual illustration of what exists and what is proposed. And, although I know of no instance in which it has been done adequately, it would not be difficult to develop an accurate and useful model, or map, as a part of the regional planning process. Only a reluctance to consider seriously the value of the visual environment appears to prevent an augmentation of regional plans that would make the visual character of distinct places within it unmistakably clear, establish the direction in which they should be developed, and show revisions with each change of the practical survey and plan.

It is useless to extend our application of the new model for scale to broader and broader fields of designing. Our brief examination of its effects upon the treatment of scale in buildings, in small towns, and in cities, has sufficed to show that it is an open system which may be applied to any kind of a design in any kind of a context. The only limitations are those imposed by our failures of imagination in designing and by our failure to comprehend the architectural context in depth. For the present, most of our designs for very large projects reveal a wide gap between what we comprehend in the abstract, and what we thoroughly know by trial and experience.

In architecture, and in urban design, our scope of designing has been enlarged through our conception of the environment as a continuum of defined space. The designer has developed a realistic way to conceive of the whole extent of the area that he is asked to control, which allows no part of the design to escape his imagination. This enlargement appears to match the joining together of the practical world through rapid transportation and communication. The treatment of architectural scale that matches this progression, shares its complexity and dynamism. On the one hand, it does not allow us to suppose that the scale of our designs can be determined by an easily applied formula. On the other hand, it holds out the promise that where there is the energy and the skill to design imaginatively our treatment of scale may be governed by an over-all conception – and environment of scale – that matches our best understanding of the world around us.

INDEX

African sculpture 45
Agra, Taj Mahal 120–2, 125, 142
Alberti, Leone Battista 10, 34, 38
An Approach to Design 58
Anatomy of the Village, The 214
Annapolis, Maryland 123
Arcadia, scale of 223–4
Architect, as an artist 173
Architectura 10
Architectural Principles in the Age of Humanism 32, 34
Architectural Review 163, 212 n, 214, 223; editors 223
Architecture of Humanism, The 104
Architecture of Japan (Drexler) 36
Aristotle 45
Athens: Parthenon 45, 50; Propylea 51, 52

Baroque architects 57, 182–3, 204
Baroque architecture: Blenheim Palace 137, 138; proportions 56–7, 152; Rome, St Ignazio 135, St Peter's 125, 130; structure 148–9; Vaux-le-Vicomte 137; Versailles 133 ill, 134, 138, 139 ill, 140; Wies 140–2; views 56–7, 182, 183 ill
Baroque Gardens 133, 134
Baroque Squares: Nancy, Copenhagen 186–7
Baroque urban scale: 182–9; between cities 188–9, 192; and space 195–6; system 186, 194, 198, 204–5
Bauhaus 10
Beauty 44–5, 48
Beaux Arts, Ecole des: 10, 24, 138; overblown scale 168, 191
Binyon, Lawrence 207
Blaser, Werner 36 n
Blenheim Palace 137–8, 142
Boston, Mass. 219
Brasilia 22 ill, 180, 195
Breuer, Marcel 137
Brick, size 15, 68
Brick, statement of 26, 75, 76, 112, 146, 147 ill, 148, 149
Brunelleschi 38
Brussels, Palais de Justice 191, 193 ill
Building laws 206

Building technology 16, 17, 73, 116, 153, 170–4
Buildings and Prospects 210 n
Budgaard, J. A. 51, 52

Castle Howard, gate 129 ill
Ceiling 65, 66 ill, 133, 140
Center City, U.S.A. 219–20
Chandigarh 180
Charlottesville, Va. 221–2
Chicago: Convention Hall (project) 172; Illinois Institute of Technology 150, 154, 171, 172; Lake Shore apartments 171
Chinese architecture 35
Chinese vases 104
Circulation diagram 198, 199
Cities in Evolution 201
City Beautiful Movement 182
City block: uncontrolled 107–10; controlled 111–14
City, mythical 204–5
City, *see also* urban
City, small 217
City Development, a study of Parks, Gardens and Cultural Institutions 209 n
Classical Revival 24, 186
Concrete, reinforced 25, 69 ill, 100, 102 ill, 103 ill, 146, 147 ill, 149
Constable, John 207, 208
Context of scale: 201–5, 210–12; Center City 219–20; Exeter 214–16; Lyme Regis 212–14; metropolitan 216–19; regional 224–5; remembered 218–19; Virginia 220–22
Copenhagen, Amalienborg Square 186
Corbusier, *see* Le Corbusier
Cotman, J. S. 208, 209
Cotswold village 81
Counter Attack 223 n
Cozens, J. R. 207
Crabshell 198, 199
Cullen, Gordon 212, 213, 214

Day, unit of size 156–7, 163–4
Delhi, Fort gate 142